Day Trading for Beginners

Want to be a Day Trader? Learn How to Trade for a Living and Discover These Powerful Day Trading Tips and Strategies in 2019

Bill Sykes

Timothy Gibbs

© **Copyright 2019 - All rights reserved.**

The content contained within this book may not be reproduced, duplicated, or transmitted without direct written permission from the author or the publisher.

Under no circumstances will any blame or legal responsibility be held against the publisher, or author, for any damages, reparation, or monetary loss due to the information contained within this book. Either directly or indirectly.

Legal Notice:

This book is copyright protected. This book is only for personal use. You cannot amend, distribute, sell, use, quote or paraphrase any part, or the content within this book, without the consent of the author or publisher.

Disclaimer Notice:

Please note the information contained within this document is for educational and entertainment purposes only. All effort has been executed to present accurate, up to date, and reliable, complete information. No warranties of any kind are declared or implied. Readers acknowledge that the author is not engaging in the rendering of legal, financial, medical, or professional advice. The content within this book has been derived from various sources. Please consult a licensed professional before attempting any techniques outlined in this book.

By reading this document, the reader agrees that under no circumstances is the author responsible for any losses, direct or indirect, which are incurred as a result of the use of information contained within this document, including, but not limited to, — errors, omissions, or inaccuracies.

Table of Contents

Introduction

Section 1: Day Trading Benefits and the Requisites

Chapter 1: Why Day Trading is a Profession to Consider

- Reasons Why People Pursue Day Trading
- Why day trading is better than buying and holding
- Ways to make money in the market
- Summary of the rest of the book

Chapter 2: The Basics of Day Trading

- Day trading terminology
- Personality traits for successful traders
- How day trading differs from other types of trading
- The most commonly used platforms for day trading
- What is there to be traded: The main day trading markets
- Risk in Day Trading
- Types of orders in Day Trading

Chapter 3: Beginner's Day Trading Essential

Information

Essential Tools

A day in the life of a Day Trader: What traders normally do every day

Formulating achievable goals and understanding common constraints

Keeping your emotions under control in day trading

Factors to be considered when beginning to trade

Section 2: Strategies

Chapter 4: The Candlestick Strategy

Chapter 5: The Trend (Momentum) Strategy

History of Momentum trading
Technical analysis tools
The variations from the main strategy
Advantages
Disadvantages

Chapter 6: The ABCD Pattern

History
Types of ABCD Patterns
Rules for trading with the ABC pattern
Advantages
Disadvantages

Chapter 7: Reversal Trading

History
Advantages
Disadvantages

Chapter 8: The Scalping Strategy
- Variations
- Scalping techniques
- Advantages
- Disadvantages

Chapter 9: Daily Pivots
- Advantage
- Limitation
- History
- Pivot points techniques

Final thoughts about strategies

Section 3: Completing Your Trade

Chapter 10: Building a Watch List

Importance of building a watchlist

How to build a stock list
- Company details
- Stock analysis

Chapter 11: Paying Attention to the Market Until the Trade is Completed

Chapter 12: Day Trading Tips for Success

Identify Key Entry and Exit Points
- Avoid Hitting and Running
- Limit Losses
- Starting Small
- Willingness to learn
- Risk only what you can afford to lose
- Be realistic
- Timing the Trades
- Discipline
- Trading Plan

Chapter 13: Learning to Begin Day Trading

with a Minimalist Approach

The benefits of minimalism

How to incorporate minimalism in your day trading approach

Chapter 14: Avoiding the Herd Mentality

Chapter 15: Reflecting on the Lessons Learned from Trading

Conclusion

References

Introduction

Any successful trader will tell you that day trading is a lot like riding a roller coaster. Though fun and exciting, it sometimes depletes your hope and takes away your will to continue. There are moments you will be extraordinarily happy, but in others, you will feel powerless. What you should know is that these low moments should not get to your head and make you panic or even quit. As in every journey you begin in life, you should be keen on how you address adversities since no one promised that there won't be hard times along the way. It is at these times that you should look into the stories of successful traders and see how they have managed to overcome such times.

Successful trading is an art and a science. Most of its aspects are those of business like any other. You obviously need to look out for the market signals, obtain as much information about the market as you can, and maintain a focus of getting a competitive edge in all markets that you participate in. Sooner or later, you'll learn that the same lessons that drive the most successful trading firms are the same lessons that drive their trading each day. Once you get it right from the beginning, every day for you will be a winning day.

In today's information age, you are bound to hear a lot about day trading from the media outlets. The complexity and variety of these voices can make it hard for you to separate the truth from the myths and misconceptions. Yet, to be a successful trader, you must get the facts right in all aspects! Some of the most common misconceptions that you need to avoid include:

Day trading is a hoax: The entire day trading business is thought of as a business of the chosen few who live off of new traders' gullibility by promoting the stock to drive their prices. Whilst there truly is a pump and dump scheme in which self-serving stock promoters drive up prices, sell, and leave the buyers staggering, this is just a small phenomenon within the entire occupation. In fact, there are always unethical dealers in every type of business who sell counterfeit products and mislead the buyers. The trick is about learning to identify and avoid such unethical traders and pursue your activities successfully. Most of the naysayers who lose their money in day trading and blame it on the occupation fail to understand that this is due to their lack of appropriate knowledge and misinformation. This doesn't make day trading a hoax.

The get-rich-quickly mentality: Rumour has it that placing a few stocks is your gate path to financial success. Truly, there are some outliers in the scene who record substantial success within a short period, but this doesn't always happen. Just as in any other business, you'll probably experience various ups and downs, and it all depends on how resilient and willing you are to learn from your mistakes. In fact, those who work their way up there through plenty of hurdles have better risk management skills, and their trading prowess is enhanced by the day.

The "must-get-rich using the basics" mentality: In reference to the above point, continuous learning exposes you to an oasis of knowledge you could never have imagined. Furthermore, the trading market is constantly changing and learning places you on the top of the trends to eventually make you the most profitable. Essentially, you will need to respond to the market changes through continuous learning. You will eventually become obsolete if you don't keep up with training.

You need huge sums of money to be profitable in the market: One of the rumors that keep people off the trading scene is that those who have made it are those who began with a lot of money. This would mean acquiring a big trading account and placing big trade positions. This is just not true. In fact, you can have a lot of money when you begin to trade and lose all of it if you don't know how to handle the market. Day trading is one of the professions you can consider as a "small business" option. Your job is to concentrate on building up your trading skills before you can think of investing a lot of your money.

Most outrageously, rumor has it that you don't need to be trained to day trade: While you technically don't need a certificate for your training, assuming that you need no education to engage in trading is one of the most common myths in day trading. Learning about the basics is important, but it's the real-life training that exposes you to aspects such as the best strategies and identifying patterns and finding a framework that works for you that matter. Saying you don't need training is setting yourself up for failure.

You can make massive amounts in a single trade: Well, true as it is, making such a dubious statement makes it look like this happens all the time, while it is certainly not the case. In fact, when you're just a beginner, perhaps with a small account, chances of such immediate massive profits are rare. The truth is that, similar to any other business, you will have to identify a workable strategy to make the wisest investment, without taking too much or too little risk.

That day trading compares to gambling is simply a myth. This is the stereotype used by the masses that do not trade or have dived into the trading scene before without good skills and failed terribly. They view trading as a gambling machine that only lets you win once, then eats away your money every other time. The truth is that trading can be like gambling if you allow it. You would allow it to be by failing to train and master the best skills.

That said, remember that you can ultimately achieve financial success through day trading, using consistent efforts and strategic trading. Entering the day trade profession is not a process to be taken lightly. There are the basic requirements for entering the trade, and there are the critical requisites that you have to observe for you to make it in day trading. For instance, you must be able to apply a workable strategy, get a lot of practice, know about the capital requirements, consider goals that you want to achieve and their constraints, choose a broker, and be in the right mental state. This book guides you through the most profound aspects of day trading.

Section 1: Day Trading Benefits and the Requisites

Chapter 1: Why Day Trading is a Profession to Consider

Reasons Why People Pursue Day Trading

The truth is, trading can be disheartening at times. Even the top achievers have some losing periods, so never be too hard on yourself. It is always good to learn about focusing on the positive side of something, lest you miss an opportunity that could mean everything to your life. Whether you are a full-time day trader or starting out part-time, there are evident reasons why you should actually engage in trading. The following offers a list of some of these reasons:

Trading gives you financial freedom: One of the most obvious reasons people want to become day traders is to improve their finances, and they think it is possible in this field. Trading gives you a chance to not just cater to personal and simple bills, but to be able to live comfortably from anywhere in the world. You have the freedom to purchase not based on what you can afford, but on what you actually want.

Trading improves your mental toughness: Clearly, day traders are people who have chosen to not follow the masses and what seems acceptable by the majority of society. They have chosen to see the world for what it really is and are ready to challenge the status quo that trading is only for the chosen elite few. That's what mentally tough people do. They have the mindset of a winner and are always ready to face a situation for what it really is, believing it's going to pay off if they stick to the journey with consistent efforts.

Trading gives you flexibility as you escape the usually 9-5 day grind: What's better than earning big and being flexible? Most of the white collar jobs that pay well require you to stay in the office from morning to evening. Day trading is among the few professions where you earn enormously from the comfort of your home or any location in the world. You can make a schedule to travel or go on vacation without having to worry about missing work. Also, it saves you from having to wake up, drive to your job, and work for 40 or more hours per week.

It makes you more knowledgeable - you gain a better understanding of the world: In trading, you are exposed to the conditions of various economies of the world. By playing around with currencies and exchange rates between countries, you remain updated about the world at all times, much more than people who do not trade. You can even identify a place to travel or relocate to by learning about its currency value.

Trading has a leveled playing field: To be a day-trader, you don't have to present a certificate to anyone to show your education level. Whether you are a college dropout or university graduate, all it takes are most of the soft skills you already know, such as diligence and commitment. In his study on the profitability of day trading, Ryu (2012) observes that most of the successful traders in the world have no formal education. Through these skills, you gain a better understanding of yourself, and you can calmly and tactfully handle all other situations around you.

Trading equips you with life-enriching skills: Life in the modern world has become increasingly demanding. People are under the pressure of meeting the various demands from their personal and work domains. The modern lifestyle has increased our chances to mold our lives the way we want by giving us a lot of opportunities and material possessions. To make our lives better, we are expected to have some crucial skills that can help us through various hurdles in our day-to-day life. These include:

Critical thinking and problem solving: While participating in the market, you take the other marketers as a single lot and attempt to figure out what they are thinking, so you can gain a competitive edge. It is through anticipating the steps of others that you can call in your shots in the trade market. These skills are not only applicable in trading but are useful in all other domains of life. You find an opportunity, think critically through it, and know how to solve a challenge.

Risk management: Trading has been a training ground for people to manage risks better since it is all about risk management. Just like the SEALs who undergo hectic training to become the best in the game, traders undergo a rough risk management training where they have to know just how much is acceptable and at what time. To be a successful trader, you have to establish the point in the market with the potential of giving you the highest ROI. Unlike in gambling where you gamble all day long, say in a casino, with your chances of winning anything is almost close to zero, day trading gives you a chance to maximize your wins all day long. This is done through proper management of your positions by being calculative about your risks. Therefore, risk management is a fundamental aspect of trading, which differentiates it from gambling.

Failure management: One of the best skills of the most successful people whose success stories we read about is failure management. They understand that failure is part of the journey, and it's what adds up to your experience. Trading exposes you to various wins and losses, and it is usually in the moments of failure that you are expected to remain mostly positive.

You learn your strengths and weaknesses: Whether it's making decisions quickly, giving up easily, or being organized, trading will sooner or later expose these traits within you. This will help you realize a part of your psychology you may have never known about. It also helps you utilize your strengths to the best and take steps to address your weaknesses.

Introspectiveness: Trading forces you to master the skill of carefully analyzing your life to learn about the things you did well and those that you did not do well, so you can improve your chances of success in the long run. This is a skill that most people struggle with, and they do not realize that some qualities are hidden under their misguided outlook of themselves.

Objectivity: To make it in trading, you are forced to always be objective. Objectivity is the pillar that keeps us from being bias from in our judgment, and we need this value to be able to trade effectively. Once we master this skill, we are able to keep away from poor judgments, and we cannot easily get frustrated in any area of our lives.

Why day trading is better than buying and holding

Most people are conflicted between buying and

holding (investing) versus day trading since the two appear to be at odds with each other. Yet the ultimate goal of every investor is to buy low and sell high. Day trading is the riskiest form of stock trading since it involves rapidly buying and selling stock to maximize on the small price changes within a day. Technically, stock trading is all about deciding beforehand on the percentage decrease you are expecting to buy and deciding beforehand the percentage increase you want to sell at. There is a fair share of risk that exists in day trading since the price of a stock may not go as you want in the timeframe anticipated.

Conversely, the buying and holding model of investment is one in which the investor buys and keeps an investment for an extensive amount of time, waiting for the value to rise. Its risk is determined by the organization's long-term prospects. Its potential risk is found if the company does not take the direction earlier anticipated and based on the price the investor bought it at.

What is outstanding about day trading is that it offers you a chance to benefit from your efforts. It enhances your autonomy and helps you become a more experienced person every day. Buying and holding for a long period of time means that you are relying on the efforts of others (a company) for you to benefit. Your profits are determined by their long term outcome. You have a passive role in the investment since you identify appropriate funds or securities and hold them up for a long time. In day trading, you have an active role since you monitor the market every day to maximize the best buying and selling times. Day trading gives you the chance to have a full-time job while buying and holding is like keeping your money in a relatively safe place, waiting for it to mature.

Besides, day trading isn't about perfection, since you can purchase stocks that recuperate support mark in capacity when you sell while buying and holding requires you to be absolutely right about a company's success. In day trading, you get quick feedback which transforms you into a better trader every day, and you can spot your woes quickly by studying charts.

Even so, day trading allows you to enjoy your money as it comes rather having to wait for an endgame that never comes by buying and holding. Day trading, as mentioned earlier, gives you the financial freedom to spend your money when you desire.

Ways to make money in the market

As highlighted earlier, a day trader has to ensure that all amounts of the specific securities are closed by the time the market is closing for the day. This means that a trader who wants to be successful must be speculative and exit a day's trade tactfully before being caught up in unimaginable risks of negative gaps in prices between two days. There are various ways through which you can make money in the day trade market, provided the trader is sound and understands just how to go about it. It can be rough because of the fast-paced action, but the necessary tools and knowledge lead to success.

For instance, successful day traders focus on establishing stocks with high betas, which refers to the condition of how fast a stock's price can go up in the market. This entails identifying the companies whose business is doing really well. Since day trading refers to trading on positions on only one day, as a trader you ought to identify the stocks that can move up and down fast, provided you are able to capture the movement and know when to execute the buy orders and when to execute the sell orders.

Also, day traders seek to identify penny stocks, which refers to the small companies' stocks, which basically have a worth of fewer than 5 dollars per share. Regardless of their size, these stocks carry a high-profit potential with them. Rather than awaiting the big companies' stocks that may not have that high of a propensity to changing in a day, a wise trader goes for the penny stocks and exits the trade in the evening with a good intraday profit.

Further, day traders increasingly embrace binary options to trade, which is done by entering a position and betting that its value will increase even though they do not own the stocks. Through the binary options, you choose a security and set the duration of time that you are going to hold the position. It offers returns in a short time, and even though you bet that the value of the security will rise, its fall does not affect you since you still make money from the market volatility using proper timing strategies.

News playing is also a basic way of acting on your position in the market. Most successful day traders rely on major news announcements to buy or sell stocks. The movement of prices triggered by such announcements is quite significant for a day trader, and the success of a trader depends on how much they had indulged in the market based on rumors which always circulate before the actual news announcements. Furthermore, traders make money through artificial intelligence, which allows technical analysis on a real-time basis and gives traders substantial knowledge about market conditions.

The reason why most people do not go for day trading or indulge in it and fail is simply that they don't have time to engage in the trade that much. Yet extensive research is what day trading entails to be able to spot the penny stocks and high beta stocks, and know exactly how to leverage them.

Summary of the rest of the book

Of course, there is no universal answer to the right time or the right way that one should be trading to reap good fruits. There are various traders out there who engage in the stock market at different levels. Some take it as a part-time gig, while others trade for a living. Day trading is not as simple as sitting down, accessing the internet, and staring at your computer screen. It requires enormous efforts that are not even guaranteed to pay off. However, even with this reality check into day trading, you can always set realistic expectations and use the right tools to achieve your goals. This is what the rest of the book is dedicated to.

It discusses the basics of day trading, the essential information you need as a beginner, the most popular and workable strategies that successful traders have always used, and the daily tips you can leverage for success. It helps you to distinguish between the best platforms and strategies that beginners use from those that suit the veterans. Also, it shows you the cost requirements for each of the commonly used platforms to ensure that the platforms you use fit your budget.

Further, it offers insight on the appropriate amount of risk that you, as a day trader, should take depending on your experience, knowledge, and the platform that you are using. It shows you the best tips and techniques that the most successful traders have used to give you a competitive edge while you engage in day trading. The common mistakes that the average or losing traders commit are explored throughout to help you omit them and prevent you from becoming the 89% of day traders who lose in the game. It also shows you the kind of mentality to avoid while day trading and the one you should embrace for your benefit instead.

Finally, it shows you why day trading is the best form of trading for you, especially if you are looking for a job rather than just making an investment and waiting for long durations. While other forms of trading are also worthwhile and they have had a great success record, the rest of the book focuses on day trading and shows you why you should select it.

Chapter 2: The Basics of Day Trading

Obviously, the first thing that traders want to know is how much money they can make from trading. Most of us have heard that day trader get a lot of money from this profession. True to this, there is plenty of profits to be earned from day trading. It is quite obvious that some traders will still need an additional job on top of day trading every month, but others can attain a comfortable lifestyle based on day trading alone. How much money you make as a trader is mainly determined by various factors including the amount of money you begin with, how much training you've invested in, the market in which you trade, your personality, and even the volatility of the market. This chapter takes you through the fundamental aspects that you are sure to need while in the day trading market.

Day trading terminology

Learning about the trading lingo offers you a secret code to the significant day trading ideas. The following is a checklist of the most significant and trading-unique terms that you should be aware of, and which are used throughout the rest of the book.

- Initial public offering (IPO): Used to refer to a firm selling a particular set of shares in the market
- Float: The number of shares available for trading from a company
- Leverage rate: The rate at which the platform you use multiplies your deposit to enhance your trading power
- Profit/loss ratio: The measure of the likelihood of a platform to generate profit as compared to a loss
- Entry and exit points: The points at which you buy and sell your position, respectively
- The Bid: The price at which a broker buys a security from a trader
- The Ask: The price the broker sells the security at
- Spread: The variance between the buying and selling price of a security by a broker
- Liquidity: identifies as the ease of a stock to be purchased and sold in the market devoid of major price effects.
- Market makers: the determinants of buy and sell orders as well as facilitating liquidity.
- Resistance level: the point at which the position holders subsumes the buyers in the market and therefore diminishes the chances of stock price rising.
- Support level: Contrasts with the resistance

level. It is the point at which buyers override the position holders, diminishing the chances of stock prices diminishing.
- Breakout level: the level beyond a security's preceding resistance point.
- Trend: the inherent direction that the price of a stock assumes. A trend can be upwards or downwards.

These terms are applicable throughout day trading to understand the general information, charts, strategy, platforms, and patterns of trading.

Personality traits for successful traders

Discipline: Good traders have taken the market to be like their workplace. They understand that discipline is core to achieving good results. It is not just about getting a strategy and assuming that all is set for trading. The markets expose you to infinite chances to trade, and yet there is only a short time that is right for you to trade. There are only a few seconds in which your chances of success in a day are optimal. Therefore, there is only a short time of actual trading. Now, discipline lets you give those few moments your maximum concentration. Should you lack discipline, you will always be distracted during the best times for you to trade. Such people are the naysayers who spread rumors that they spend the whole day on the computer trading and they only incur losses. Yet it is during the most crucial moments that they were distracted. At a time when social media has become part of daily life for most of us, it is easy to get distracted in the world of the internet and lose sight of your stops for the day.

A good trader is disciplined and follows their schedule, and they are able to act instantaneously when trading opportunities occur.

Adaptability: In the trading market, there are hardly two days that are similar. Today there is high volatility, but tomorrow the volatility might be low. If you strictly follow an example as if it were an exam that you are about to sit for, you are bound to fail. You need to learn to be flexible and take each day as it comes. You need to be able to implement suitable strategies for all types of market conditions and know exactly which strategy fits which condition. A good trader is one who acts real-time, knows when to step aside and watch, and when to dive right in and trade. Failure to become adaptable is one way of setting yourself up for failure.

Patience: Now we know that trading is just like starting a business. You do not expect to begin making lump sums right when you first begin. It is only in a few cases that these exceptional gains do occur for a new trader. Being successful takes a lot of patience and consistent efforts as you wait for success. But basically, day trading entails a lot of waiting.

Furthermore, we already know that there are bad days, even for the very experienced traders. You need to have the patience of waiting for tomorrow, and even if tomorrow doesn't work, the next day might. Also, you need to learn to wait for the great market entering times, lest you enter too early or too late. In day trading, patience goes hand in hand with discipline, since patience allows you to wait for the time you should enter the market and discipline ensures that you are actually set to enter the market without hesitation. Typically, patience is among the greatest trading personality traits.

Forward thinking: You can't be dwelling on the past if you are a day trader. While it is paramount to use historical data to make trading decisions, you must be able to apply the information in the present day and time. You cannot buy a security at a particular price and then ignore all the market price data that changes within 10 minutes. You must be like a chess player - one who is already planning their next move tactfully based on what the opponent, in this case, the market, does, and also is able to anticipate the opponent's response to that. You keep considering the various scenarios that may play out in order to be able to implement a plan under the different scenarios.

Practice forward thinking by considering what needs to happen for you to enter a market, and what might happen when you're there; for instance, if the prices go up or down fast against you or the prices do not move, consider how you should react in each scenario.

Trading is all about knowing that each step you take brings a particular result, and being equipped with the ability to foretell.

Mental toughness: As mentioned in the reasons you should trade section, day trading in so many ways forces you to be mentally tough. But we know that people quit trading all the time, saying that it is not their thing, it is something for the elite few, they don't seem to be getting it, and all sorts of negative things. This is because they have refused to be mentally tough. Day trading requires you to be mentally tough. Mentally tough individuals never quit. They never give in to pressure no matter how competitive the playing ground is. They never allow the failure of one day to discourage them from continuing with the journey. In fact, they take failure as a good chance to learn and become smarter. They are thick skinned and are always ready to take any blows the trading market may throw at them. Most importantly, they are smart and curious enough to know the most appropriate risks that they should take. Making it in day trading requires you to understand that there are losing days, but they should not discourage you. It requires you to remain positive under all circumstances, and losses shouldn't deter your judgment since this will most definitely lead to more failures, and you will eventually quit having not explored your optimal potential.

Independence: Independence goes hand in hand with forward thinking. While you get some help from your mentors and books initially, day trading requires you to eventually become independent using the knowledge you have accumulated.

Finally, as a trader, there is the need to be open-minded, persistent, and decisive. You need to expect any kind of result when you trade, but you have to be consistent with your efforts despite having a loss as your result. Most importantly, you need to be decisive so that you can promptly act upon the trading opportunities when they arise.

How day trading differs from other types of trading

The most popular trading model that any newbie in the trading scene will be introduced to is buying and holding. The trader buys stocks and holds them, and the investment increases in value over a long period of time. Usually, the long-term wait is met by positive results which could even be augmented through dividends and reinvesting the profits. While some traders go for the buy and hold approach, others prefer to enter and exit the market on the same day, while still others prefer to use other approaches that outdo the former.

Thus, besides the buy and hold approach, other approaches include:

Position trading: This is a trading approach in which the traders are free to utilize both long and short term trading techniques, as they anticipate gaining from longer-term trends than those of day trading. Basically, position trading takes a span that ranges from months to years. Decisions to trade are made based on weekly and monthly price market results. While it resembles the buying and holding approach, traders in this method are not restricted to long-term only.

Swing trading: This is an approach which follows a generally short-term path since positions are held for days or weeks. Traders using this approach anticipate gaining from short-term pricing fluctuations. What mostly determines when the trader's exit is if the scheduled time is up, when a target is reached, or when the market is fluctuating contrary to the trader's expectations. This approach suits traders who are not able to be active in all trading sessions, since it does not require you to always be there. Therefore, this approach differs from day trading because even though it operates in the short term, positions can go for days without exiting the market.

Scalp trading: This is a method of trading that involves a shorter span than that of day trading. Traders buy and sell actively within seconds and minutes. It follows the business sales strategy, which reduces the selling price to make more sales because every position gives a low margin return. As such, traders in this market often buy various positions to accumulate the little profit gains obtained from each position. Additionally, they seek the lowest trading commissions lest all their profits are taken away in the commissions.

High-Frequency Trading (HFT): This trading technique entails high-frequency trades. It is perhaps the riskiest, most complex, and involved style of trading, which demands speed and attention on a 24-hour basis. Traders using this technique rely on analyzing multiple markets concurrently for profits. Successful traders in this segment are able to evaluate their composite and trademarked systems of trading. Usually, a beginner, perhaps working from home, is usually not competitive in this market. This trading approach differs from day trading since day trading follows a one market approach.

Essentially, day trading differs from all these trading mechanisms because of the holding period of the stocks bought. Remember that trading mainly entails buying low and selling high. Also, remember that day trading entails entering and exiting the market within the same day. Day trading is often like a full-time job, where you have to identify and ensure that all requisites are in order. Any disruptions of the working space can make traders miss the intraday price fluctuations, and hence miss their best trading opportunities. However, it is not as complex, intensive, or risky as scalp trading, which takes less trading spans and stricter conditions.

The most commonly used platforms for day trading

When you are a newbie or a veteran who has realized they need a change, you might get confused when choosing a strategy, platform, and market to enter in day trading. However, you may have a rough idea of what you want in a platform, for instance. It is a no brainer that you want premium research, low costs, a comprehensive platform, and innovative tools for trading. There are various brokers for trading out there, with every platform trying to attract as many traders as possible. The most commonly used platforms include:

Trade station: This platform is number one when it comes to trading technology through its web-based technique. It is actually the ultimate go-to option for many future investors and active traders. It equips traders with information gathering capabilities through access to a large database. Studies and charts that have been accumulated over a long period of time are available in this platform. Furthermore, these studies can easily be adjusted to fit user specifications using the platform's easy coding language.

Interactive Brokers: With its ability to cater to active trade, Interactive Brokers is generally preferred among day traders. While the platform has no allowance for newbies, it sure has hotkeys and special orders for placing any kind of trade. It also has margins ranging from low to high to cater to traders of all levels of risk tolerance. That said, IB offers the lowest commissions in the industry, and thus, it is common in the institutional community day trading.

Ameritrade: This platform is popular for its variety of tools which help traders in their day to day activities. It offers access to analysis of earnings, charts, and even backtesting. Traders are able to analyze stocks on a real-time basis and share layouts of their workspaces. Also, this platform gives access to above-average commissions and services. It is useful for anyone ranging from active and experienced traders to newbies.

Charles Schwab: This platform has progressively created a positive image in the trading scene through its delivery of high-quality customer service. It has a wide range of features that makes its interaction with the trader easy and worthwhile. It also has a lot of Exchange Trade Funds (ETFs) without high commissions. It allows access to a wide research base, and a trader far from lacks any information they need. However, this platform has high trade commissions that any trader wants to consider before committing.

Lightspeed: This is one of the most favorable platforms for beginners. It allows one to trade with simply the click of a button. It allows a high level of personalization, whereby you can put as many as four modules allowing you to access and join different pieces of information suitable for your trading strategy. You can also make a shortcut key to take you directly to the page you want to keep monitoring. However, the platform has a price that many newbies may not be comfortable with, but it also has demos that one can try before committing to the fees.

Ally Invest: This is another one of the go-to platforms for active traders because of its good charting, analytical tools, and even researching offered for free. Also, it has low commissions, and the account has no minimum, giving the trader a chance to plan for their money no matter the amount. However, Ally has been discredited on various occasions for the lack of branches that can offer traders a wide range of alternatives, and the lack of mutual funds for transaction-fee.

Of course, there are many more platforms, including eOption and Fidelity, but these are less popular. In fact, Interactive Brokers and Trade Station are the most popular platforms. Nerdwallet provides a comprehensive review of these platforms to give traders an easy chance of getting their options right when choosing a platform. Those that meet the criteria of flexibility, standard fee, and access to information are most notably Interactive Brokers, Trade Station, and Lightspeed.

What is there to be traded: The main day trading markets

The stock market, Forex, and futures are all major markets in day trading. Others, such as options, are prevalent as well. Options, however, is most suitable for Swing traders who have their positions for weeks, not an active day trader.

The following is a brief overview of each:

Stock market: This is perhaps the most popular market that crosses the mind when one thinks about trading. This market allows ETFs and shares of companies to be traded under various opportunities, which include spread betting. This opportunity, for instance, allows you to gain even if the prices may be falling. Positions in this market are best attained at news release or financial reports, and from studying the practical signs. Further, all positions are exited at the end of each day at a particular time. There has to be an equity balance of at least 25,000 dollars. The implication of this to new traders is that they should begin by setting aside 30,000 dollars to trade.

Forex: Now, Forex is the largest market across the globe. It is highly accessible and allows trading for the whole day. It appeals to day traders because of its massive volume. It contains multiple opportunities for trading with high liquidity, which makes the opening and closing of positions relatively quick.

What is more appealing even for beginners is that they can start with capital as low as 100 dollars, although about 1000 dollars is the ideal recommended amount. The mainstay of this market is that one currency is exchanged for another. In this exchange, there is the term called currency pair, which entails the amount that, say, the US dollar is exchanged for another, say, Canadian dollar.

That said, every trading platform has its own requirements for Forex trading, and this is the point where a trader thinking to enter the Forex trade should be most careful. One should make demos to their friend to practice and learn. Profits in this market are earned from speculating how the price of one currency will move relative to another.

Futures: As its name suggests, Futures is a market which mainly focuses on future prices. A buyer and a seller agree to buy or sell a particular amount of a commodity or security at a later date. Day traders benefit from the intraday price fluctuations between the duration of the contract during the day. Futures requires less capital than stocks, but more capital than Forex. With about 3,500 dollars you can trade in Futures, where you can get Futures contracts such as S & P Emini. Different contracts give rise to different official market hours. The trick for a day trader is to keep tabs on the particular contract's official hours to know the right time to exit a market.

Also, specific day trading platforms have different requirements for Futures trading, and this should be an important factor for consideration.

Binary Options: Although less popular, this is perhaps the simplest market in which a trader knows in advance the timing and the returns of a successful position. This sector is seemingly booming, and regulations are changing. Remember that laws surrounding a market are a major consideration when you're thinking of getting into trading. Another factor to consider while trading in this market is if the asset you are trading will rise or drop in value. Understanding these dynamics is not difficult, considering the potential outcome is known beforehand. Binary options offer a unique day trading experience and can even contribute to traders' portfolio of the day.

Cryptocurrencies: Cryptocurrencies have become the talk of the day when it comes to trading. It is a market that has attracted many investors and became a great source of finances in the recent past, with the most popular currencies being Bitcoin and Ethereum. There are minimal entry barriers, and the market is relatively easy to trade, even for beginners.

Commodities: This market simply entails the trading of foodstuffs, minerals, and even oil.

Risk in Day Trading

Risk management is among the fundamental lessons learned in trading. You must learn how to manage your money because, after all, it is not worth it to trade if you'll run broke after your first month in the venture. The most successful traders are those who know how to manage the different types of risks prevalent in day trading, with the greatest being the financial risk.

Financial risk: As the mother of all risks in day trading, traders must be careful about the volatility of the market prices, in which fluctuations can make one lose terribly. It is hard to benefit when a market moves in the negative direction by a large margin. Furthermore, there are few opportunities being preyed upon by too many traders. In cases such as this, it's always best to be careful whenever entering trading, and also entering a position on a particular day. Especially for newbies, it is recommended that they do not place huge amounts of cash into a single trade since this can discourage them from going on. Market information is paramount in avoiding financial risk.

Capital risk: There are various upfront costs associated with trading, including the software, infrastructure, and news services. There are other ongoing expenses in every platform, including commissions or ECN, interests, charting packages, as well as communication charges. You don't want to indulge in a venture where you will lose all the money you've invested. Also, you don't want to engage in a platform where all you'll be doing is paying for the ongoing expenses without really getting the value for your money.

Mental risk: Trading is perhaps the most addictive

form of gambling, and with a trader's intelligence being enhanced day by day, they are much more likely to get addicted. One might wonder, why not be on their trading spot all the time and earn a lot of cash, provided they are good at it? It may look interesting, and you may be tempted to think that it is good for you, but in the long run, being addicted to trading exposes you to adverse mental risk. After all, the main aim of day trading is for you to have the financial freedom to do other things. If you do not take time off, when will you ever enjoy your money? Remember that too much work without play always makes one a dull person. You should control how much trading you do in a day, or how much space trading occupies in your mind. Do not invest in a venture that will give you financial freedom but a lifetime of mental bondage.

Types of orders in Day Trading

While placing a trade order seems as simple as clicking a "buy" or a "sell" button when it's time to do so, executing orders requires maximum attention to the various types of orders and knowing exactly what to do every time you are in the market. Each of the order serves a significant purpose.

The following is a checklist of trade orders that you should pay attention to in order to avoid slipping and losing:

Market order: This is perhaps the simplest in the trading market. It has a buying and a selling option. Usually, the trader has no control over the buying or selling price of the market order. The market gives you the prevailing price, and that is what you get. It is preferable at times when traders are in need of entering or exiting positions, but can be dangerous since you may buy at the ask price and sell at the bid price, or experience a large negative difference. The ask price is the one that sellers that are willing to sell to you have, and the bid price is the one that the willing buyers place.

Limit order: Likewise, there is a buy and sell limit order. It is a directive to purchase or give away a position at a specific price, different from the current price in the market. It gives allowance to the traders to trade at a preferable price, be it buying or selling. A buy limit order, for instance, allows a buyer to set a limit beyond which they can't buy shares. For instance, if the current price of a stock is 10 dollars, a trader may choose to set a limit of 8 dollars, and only when the price of the willing sellers hits 8 or below can the trader execute the order. A sell limit order, on the other hand, allows the trader to set a limit below which they can't sell an order to prevent them from making losses. A limit order is more preferable to market order when the trader has a lot of time to wait for the order, but the market order is considered more efficient just when the trader wants to execute orders quickly.

Stop order: This is a buy or sell order which is designed to help prevent losses for the investor. It is generally considered useful for long positions, but can also serve as stop-losses for short positions. A buy stop order, for instance, is one that is placed above the prevailing market price; hence, the order is executed at or above that stop price. Once the stop is reached, a buy stop order becomes more or less like the market order since the trader is given any price, and now they can stop before the prices move too contrary to their expectations. A sell stop order can be leveraged to exit a long trading position. Orders are filled when the price is at or below the stop point. Upon reaching the sell stop, the order is executed at the amount buyers are willing to give, just like in a market order, preventing impending losses when the prices are moving against the trader.

The major limitation with stop orders is that one cannot be sure of the buying or selling price they will receive. For that reason, there is the stop-limit order as described below.

Stop-limit order: This directive is almost comparable with the one above (stop), only that it has a boundary which prevents it from acting like the market order once the stop is reached. Clearly, it has the features of both the stop and the limit order. In this order, the trader sets two price points, the stop, and the limit price. It begins as a stop order, but upon reaching the stop, it turns into a limiting value directive. It gives the trader a degree of security to exit the positions if they suspect any impending losses and also allows them to set the price at which they prefer to buy or sell stocks.

Trailing stop order: This order has many similarities with the stop order, only that the stop order has a specific price that it targets for the order to be executed, while the trailing stop order allows a trader to set their preferred change in the prevailing prices. Traders use it to exit short positions, even though it is generally considered appropriate for long positions.

Chapter 3: Beginner's Day Trading Essential Information

Essential Tools

Infrastructure: Day trading is just like any other profession that requires infrastructure to enable it to run. Technology has made trading easy because traders have access to most of the equipment they need, which includes computers or laptops, modems, routers, mobile phone with internet connectivity, and great communication capability. Also, traders need some specialized software to keep tabs on every activity going on in the market all day long.

The active traders who have made day trading their full-time job acquire Electronic Communication Networks (ECN) such as SelectNet and Instinet to keep up with all the market activities. Having this software exempts traders from having to pay a fee for every trade to the brokers since they can solely access all information concerning their position. These ECNs are normally free but to join and use any, membership must be approved. They prefer this to get ECN capabilities to monitor the market. Alternatively, some traders, especially those who trade occasionally, use online brokerage accounts, whose major drawback is that it incurs more costs.

Such infrastructure requires some dollars every month. However, it is important to note that using the brokerage approach incurs you more costs and exposes you to the risk of getting delayed information. Yet in day trading, it is the little expense details that determine the difference between success and failure in becoming profitable.

Capital

The principles of day trading are applicable for all markets, including stock, commodities, and options, but the capital requirements vary for each market. As mentioned, and even as a basic rule of nature, you need capital for you to engage in trade. Hence, if you are thinking of starting up, you must set aside capital to start and be a reasonable risk taker, lest you lose it all. Be sure to have your initial capital outlay get you somewhere concerning your trading goals.

Some of the capital requirements reflect in commissions for the Direct Access Brokers. Commissions are computed on the basis of the volume of shares being traded. Whenever getting in and out of a position, you have to consider the corresponding commission charges. Some brokers ask for high commissions, while others are considered cheaper.

Other costs are incurred in the spread, which refers to the difference between the prices at which quick buyers get securities and the prices at which quick sellers sell their securities. Essentially, a trader must have the capital to be able to take bids. Also, as discussed in the infrastructure section above, all traders need market information, and they must be able to pay for it to access.

Information

Information is perhaps the single most significant tool that you need in day trading. Remember that you are relying on every slight price movement for you to make a move.

Whilst you are not really concerned with the intrinsic value of the companies whose stock you are trading on, you are definitely concerned with how these stocks interplay with others in the market.

Using special software, internet connectivity, and computers, day traders are able to perform technical analysis and compare historical price movements with the current to make a decision. They need to access charts and to also know how to interpret those chartings to their benefit.

Time commitment

As earlier mentioned, day trading is one of the trading options that can easily become a full-time job. To benefit from this trading, you have to be sure that you can commit up to 10 hours per day in the market, either trading or preparing to trade. You definitely need to maintain your focus on the market conditions to identify any short-term opportunities. You must research for the most recent news and ongoing news stories, including regulations and earnings reports that can potentially impact your profitability.

The right personality

Personality matters a lot when it comes to day trading. As mentioned earlier, a day trader is assured of benefiting in the long run if they are disciplined, consistent with their efforts, patient, and even tough-minded. Day trading is not for the faint-hearted. One has to be ready to embrace any results and move on to try what the next day has to offer. Also, one has to realize that profits do not come by the first time of trading. It takes time and effort to accumulate experience and trade like a pro.

A day in the life of a Day Trader: What traders normally do every day

Just like in any other business, mistakes keep happening in day trading. These include errors as simple as clicking on the wrong tab, say buy instead of sell, or placing a wrong position. Other errors come forth when the trader is bombarded with information surrounding the trade, which further causes panic. In this connection, it is paramount to have a proper schedule for pre, during, and post-trade to minimize the chances of errors. Active day traders begin their day following a plan that they intend to maintain for the whole day. Although every trade is different, the following is a checklist of what should be in your daily plan:

Pre-trade:

- Check the economic calendar

Any big events in the economy can potentially affect your trade because the economy influences the prices in the market. The wise traders avoid being in trade at the time surrounding high impact economic events since anything can happen. The market typically opens at 9:30 a.m. ET. Hence, a wise trader catches up with any events that happened overnight or are coming up in the day that could affect their trade before this time. To see economic events, check the DailyFX economic calendar for Forex trade, Bloomberg for stocks, and the Yahoo! Finance earnings Calendar for individual company stocks to ensure the company has no major announcements or significant earning changes in that day. Since most of the traders participate in Forex and Futures markets, which are "around-the-clock" markets, traders can expect price rises before the market fully opens at 9:30 a.m. ET.

- Launching the workstation

After checking and taking note of what the analysts

have to say, day traders then head on to their workstation and launch the platform. A wise trader checks if the platform is working seamlessly by ensuring that quotes are streaming in smoothly from the brokers. Since there is an interplay of various technological devices and software involved here, traders spend a few moments checking that everything is functioning properly.

- Be sure to trade in the correct account

It is possible for a day trader to have a great trading day and realize in the evening that they have been trading in a simulated account instead of the real account with real capital. A beginner especially should be very cautious, since most will have the simulated account. Also, for a market such as Futures, be sure to trade with the highest volume contract and check to see the ones whose deadlines are over.

- Note down significant texts

It is good to note down any scheduled high impact news releases as a constant reminder. In fact, you should include it in your chart at the approximate time it is bound to happen. It is entirely human nature to become too indulged in trade and end up forgetting such significant events.

- Checking strategies

Check the automated orders such as stop orders and stop limit orders to ensure they are set correctly, since failure to do this may give you some of the most unwanted results. If you are using a robot to trade, ensure that all settings are correct to avoid mishaps. You already know by now that even if you are trading manually, you can have some automated orders as well; hence, this is a necessary step.

- Check to position

This is especially a critical step for traders who use default position size. Errors could include an extra zero added to or removed from the actual position, which leads to a messed up trading session. Also, note your account balance to ensure that your market entry point and any stop order that you may set are well covered. Also, be sure that when positioning, you do it correctly to minimize the potential risk. Keep in mind the most amount of risk that you want to take in a particular day.

- Self-reminder

It is good to set a few moments to go through the situations under which you've made mistakes in the past. This helps you to avoid committing the mistakes again if such situations arise again

- Scanning the market for potential opportunities

When you are all set, everything is working properly, and you are mentally prepared to handle the day, hover over the market to identify the potential opportunities to trade. You can use the technical indicators option on the chart in your market for easy establishment of what's happening. Some traders have acquired market scanning software which identifies positions which meet their targets.

Conducting this assessment guides you on how to enter the market and start trading. In days with a high volatility tendency, you would expect a higher profit margin than when the volatility is stringent.

Early trading

The first few minutes of trading are technically volatile, so you want to give the market some time to balance and avoid being rudely stopped out of a position you may set. Traders then practice the waiting game at this moment until intuition can tell them to go ahead, based on their plans, experience, and observation of prevailing market price movement. In very short holding periods, which also means less profit expected, timing must be carefully done to jump in and trade during any opportunity. Remember that seconds make a huge difference in trading.

Now, this is the time you submit orders to the market, either in the state of market price orders or stop limit orders or any other depending on your goals. Whilst some traders prefer to enter simultaneous positions, others prefer to wait until one position closes to enter another.

In the time towards lunch is when traders become extra vigilant to check if their positions have reached the target, since the period after lunch is normally less eventful. High volatility and volume of trade gradually diminish towards midday. Essentially, therefore, the successful day traders are highly active during the morning and late-morning sessions.

Second wind

This represents the period after lunch to the time the market closes at 4 p.m. ET. Institutional traders come back from lunch hour and activity resumes, allowing traders a chance to look out for some more opportunities.

Traders continue monitoring their positions taken in the morning phase and now since they all have to close before 4pm. They are very alert to jump into any opportunity once their targets are reached before the close of the market. Also, traders rarely enter a position past their own limit time, say 3 or 3:30 p.m., to allow time for exiting properly without exposing themselves to losing risks.

As 4pm draws nearer, traders close the remaining positions and cancel orders that have not been filled. Leaving any open orders can cause huge losses, since they may automatically get filled without the notice of the traders.

This is just another day at the office, where you leave having broken even, experienced a loss, or gained a profit. To the successful and enthusiastic traders, the results of the day do not really matter. They look forward to what happens tomorrow and the accumulated events over time.

Post-market time

After closing the markets, traders review their day's activities, noting down what went well and what didn't, what worked and what failed, and their mistakes during the day. This helps them to note what can be improved for the sake of tomorrow. The more organized traders maintain a journal where they note down every trade and all its details, including whether it was a success or a loss. It is important to note that a journal provides a good framework for a trader hoping to elevate their trading efforts. It is also a good motivator to actually see that you have made some wins, and you can surely win again. Traders also go through financial news to get a review of the day's activity and plan for the next day. Finally, the trader shuts down their workstation and gets time off to rejuvenate and refresh for the next day.

Ideally, most of the time of a day trader's day is spent studying and seeking to understand the market and enhance their skills using simulations. Almost all traders had experienced a time when they traded for $1000 when they actually meant to trade for $100, but all this is part of a trader's development. A proper daily schedule that is well followed is what leads to success eventually for a beginner.

Formulating achievable goals and understanding common constraints

Having learned what day trading entails and the daily activities of a trader, you would think that perhaps pulling out an excel sheet and listing how much money you need to make each day to reach your goals is the way to go. In fact, this is the case for most traders. They cannot be blamed, because our society has taught us from our childhood that when you grow up, you work for a fixed amount of time for a particular amount of pay. However, one of the greatest lessons you learn as a trader is that the trading market does not really care about your daily or weekly or even monthly targets.

Day trading is complex, and setting a subjective goal does not really work. That said, I think that attempting to make profits, since this is the ultimate goal of every trader, without clear goals is like starting a journey without knowing the destination. Therefore, despite the complexity, you have to make (realistic) goals as a trader.

The first thing you should get off your mind is the employee's perception of work, where you think you ought to earn a certain amount after working for a certain amount of time. This mentality will have you placing trades even when conditions are not favorable as you try to get ahold of targets. This will frustrate you.

Second, when setting the goal per trade, try as much as possible to be realistic by matching your targets with the market conditions. Remember that setting realistic goals increases your chances of winning, and it is often the small wins that motivate you to keep going.

Also, relate your fixed goals per trade to the amount of risk that you have taken. For instance, setting a profit goal of about 30,000 dollars if you risked about 10,000 dollars is pretty reasonable. Over time and through a chain of trades, you are likely to get 3 times your capital investment and lower losses. Remember that you must account for losses. Since it is not good to over-focus on the negative side, the losses, it is good to consider them in your goal.

Also, relate your goal to the amount of volatility in the market. Volatility describes the number of price fluctuations in the market. High volatility translates into an equally big profit or loss margin. In low volatility conditions, the profit margin is likely to be low, and so is the loss margin. If you are sure of your strategy, timing, and position, you can set a higher goal in higher volatility, only you ought to be keen on the price movements.

Your goal should relate to the strategy that you are using and the platform. Every platform has different rules and techniques for trading. Based on the platform you operate on, you should be able to set a reasonable goal. If you aren't careful, you might set unreasonable targets that your brokerage platform may not produce.

Another tip to consider when setting trading goals is your mental status. Psychological issues inhibit clear thinking and prevent one from executing their technical trading strategy properly.

What differentiates between amateur traders and veteran consistent traders when it comes to making goals per trade is the factors considered when setting a target. Take it as a rule of thumb to refrain from looking for a quick fix, but instead work through your journey the right way. It is recommended that you use a simulation program to help guide you on how to set reasonable goals for each trade (Abdolmohammadi & Sultan, 2002). By observing your various outcomes from the strategies used in the simulation account, you are able to determine the potential amount of profit you can make from a trade. Also, be sure to use the simulation strategy in a demo account to be sure about your decisions.

Maintain a journal where you record your goals in the past, say, 2 months, against what you actually achieved. If you notice an improvement trend in your results, know that you are on the right track and that you need to implement the efforts you have been using consistently. Day trading is technically meant to be more risk-averse compared to other forms of trading since stops and profits are discovered in short, quick spans. Success in day trading goals depends on the ability of a single trader to execute orders sensibly when chances arise. You should strive as much as you can to focus on the process and not the results, to learn the plan that works for you and has probably worked for your mentors, and to be careful in analyzing the prevailing market conditions.

Keeping your emotions under control in day trading

Trading can be such a hugely emotional experience. One moment you are gaining, the next you are losing terribly. Day trading is fast paced, and there are many different kinds of orders to execute. If one is not careful, they may end up making their trading decisions based on emotions and not facts. Yet this is among the most detrimental things you can do in day trading. Also, the lack of a balance in emotions makes you become frustrated and quit sooner.

Humans are not by any means technical calculators, and sometimes our moves often become misplaced. Yet day trading has been proven to be a large cash machine if well utilized. The aspect of attracting profitability and sustaining the course requires a stable steering wheel, which is why you should be sure to leave emotions far from the trading station. It means being able to maximize your gains, minimize losses, and maintain mental fortitude to have strategies for both ways. The emotionally stable traders are always strategic, disciplined, and motivated, and they aren't simply gambling while in the market. They make conscious decisions to be as rational as possible. Gambling is what most people do while in trading, where they make decisions based on their emotions and cross their fingers instead of relying on their brain.

That said, emotional times will arise, be it in moments of victory or moments of losses. Your emotions will become involved at times. However, it is by being able to silence the inner monologue that you will attain stability on the ground. Doing so will not only earn you a sense of satisfaction in your job, but it will also mean that you are on track to getting higher profits. Rely on analytics alone and not feelings!

Factors to be considered when beginning to trade

There are various crucial factors for consideration for a beginner as they begin to trade. These include choosing platforms, strategies, and styles.

To identify the best platform for you to trade in, you should seek to understand the necessary conditions needed for you to succeed. For instance, Lightspeed is the platform with the highest potential to customize, Trade Station has the best tools for trading, and Interactive Brokers has the fairest costs for traders to maximize gains.

The most essential attribute of a day trading platform is the speed through which searching for information and the implementation of orders are done. Also, a good platform is one which offers a standard fee that does not change after a month or two. There are platforms which are made seemingly attractive by the promos, and it is easy for a trader to fall for the usually appealing promos which fade in a short while and leave traders frustrated. Also, a good platform should be able to access stocks from various places in the world and not be limited to just one country. If you opt for one that does not have further options, you are limiting your chances to benefit. Further, a good platform should be easy to use and easy to integrate with the services you are using.

Also, when choosing the ideal broker, you need to consider the speed of execution, in which you're sure the platform you settle for does not restrict you from getting the price you want when you need it. Cost minimization is also paramount for a day trader since you will most definitely be entering various positions and you need the lowest possible commission rates and fees. Furthermore, be sure that your broker is properly regulated and they are legally obliged to care for your finances. Your broker also needs to be able to offer you support whenever you require it since you can be sure of needing assistance from time to time. Thus, the platform needs to have strong customer support. Your ideal leverage and margins should also be present in the chosen platform. As explored in *the various day trading platforms* section above, you should carefully choose that which suits your overall plan, and which maximizes your utility.

You ought to keep in mind that in the trading market, there is nothing that comes for free. In fact, you might want to assume that a platform with lower trading costs translates into less quality, fewer tools, ease of use, and mobile phone unfriendliness. In any case, you should be able to have around or more than $25,000 to assume a normal trading pattern.

Also, factors to be considered when selecting the style of trading that suits you include the amount of time that you can devote to trading, your risk forbearance levels, your level of experience, the size of your account, and your personality. Are you really patient? Are you a fast learner? Are you generally tough-minded? All these are factors for consideration which allow you to have a positive trading experience, and help you benefit from trading greatly.

Section 2: Strategies

For most people, strategies are used in businesses to give business operations a sense of direction. However, most people ignore the fact that strategies are an important part of our everyday lives. They enable you to live your life in order and achieve even the simplest of goals. Basically, any journey undertaken without a strategy does not have an actual blueprint for addressing the various elements of the journey. The significance of workable strategies cannot be underestimated when it comes to day trading. They form the framework under which the market can be studied, and traders leverage the most lucrative chances of making profits. In all day trading strategies, there is a need for in-depth technical analysis to establish the patterns of the price movements through charts and the different indicators for different strategies. The basic tenet of a day trading strategy is that emotions should be out of the strategy development process. Every strategy chosen should be based on facts, and there are various factors to be considered when choosing any strategy.

Chapter 4: The Candlestick Strategy

Originally established by Muhenisa Homma in the 18th century, the Japanese candlestick strategy has been in the trading scene for a long time. It was originally used by the Japanese rice merchants for market analysis, to help them predict and achieve trading power. Since then, it has passed the test of time and was reintroduced into the financial market scene 3 decades ago by Steve Nison. This way, the strategy became a standard analysis tool for the financial market. Should it have been fake, it would have become obsolete long ago, but it is significant now more than ever. To understand how exactly you can use the candlestick strategy for your benefit in your day trading endeavor, I believe it is paramount to understand its usage since its inception.

Muhenisa used candlesticks for charting and tracking the contracts for rice. Whilst everyone else was taking the same approach, Muhenisa took an emotional tactic to analyze the greed, fear, and the herd mentality, which prevented most people from joining the trade due to the widespread norms. Muhenisa sought to embrace the trade risk and benefit from it early enough. By observing the behavior of his counterparts, the masses, Muhenisa earned himself a competitive advantage since he was able to manipulate those behaviors. He did this by tracing the opening and closing prices as well as the low points and high points of the day. By placing the traces on a chart, he was able to perform a critical analysis of a day's market. The graphic representation of the columns that looked like candlesticks led to the development of the name "candlestick strategy."

Ideally, Muhenisa proved that there could be order in a market that looked so complex and chaotic. He formed an insightful basis of why prices behaved the way they did in the market. The consistent patterns became his framework for his future success in the market. Reports indicate that he made massively profitable trades.

The 1989 remaking of the candlestick strategy by Steve Nison was what brought the framework to the Western World. More traders joining the scene embraced the strategy. It has been described as a significant winning tool for day traders alongside technical analysis knowledge. As a beginner, it is easy to get lost in the variety of technical indicators in the scene, but adopting a minimalist approach is recommended. You only have to master about 2 or 3 indicators and understand them. You should have an indicator for trending and for ranging.

Going forward, a candlestick chart is used for technical analysis by the active traders. A candle can represent one minute, day, week, or even months' worth of trading action.

Each candle has a different pattern depending on the trend of the market. For instance, a green candle indicates that the traders are in control of the trade since the market opens at low prices and close on high prices, and it is also called a bullish candle. A red candle, on the other hand, represents the situation where the traders are price takers since the market opens on high prices and closes on low prices, and it is also known as a bearish candle.

Also, a morning/evening star candle is one which represents the points of reversal of a trend. They are made from long, small, and a third long bearish or bullish candle. Also, there is a rising/falling wedge which describes a candlestick formation that has extended durations. Traders use them to establish the continuation of a longer-term trend. Finally, a Doji candle is one which signals consolidation or impending breakout.

What traders are advised to pay attention to are the indicators of changes in trends in the market stock and the movement for each candle.

Patterns of candlestick strategy that work

Some of the seemingly crazy names used in the chart were developed by Muhenisa as he sought a way to make sense of the patterns. He wanted to link the tag of war between traders in the market by making a visual concept of the chart. The hanging man, the Harami, the Evening star, Doji, and the abandoned baby were the names he gave to the various high and low points of a typical trading day as indicated by his chart. Even though some have been translated into English because of its widespread use in the 21st century, the same pattern of high and low points remain.

Candlestick patterns do not all work equally. Some

patterns have been de-popularized by the portfolio managers who use algorithms to alter the functioning of the patterns. They use technical software to take advantage of traders seeking high-odds outcomes in the bearish and bullish models. Yet based on the conventional way of working, traders can study the various tradable patterns that continue to arise. That said, the following are a few patterns that work:

The three line strike: In this pattern, three downward trend candles are engulfed by a reversal pattern with three lines. After the engulfing three candles, the fourth bar opens in a lower position but reverses in a much higher position than the first series candle. This pattern has proven a high level of accuracy through the reversals.

Two black gapping: In an uptrend with a prominent top and a gap down that has two bars with weaker low, the 2 black gapping appears right after it. This pattern shows the potential of a deteriorating downward trend through more lowering of prices. The accuracy of this pattern is above average, and it is something that day traders want to look out for.

3 black crows: This is a reversal pattern which happens close to the highest high of an uptrend. It has 3 bars which record lower lows, and it is a signal that the downward trend will continue deeper. It has an above average accuracy that traders watching out for momentum plays may be trapped inside it.

The evening star: This is a bearish pattern that begins

with a tall candle which records a new high in an upward trend. The next bar records a higher point, and it produces a narrow pattern of the candlesticks since new buyers do not appear at this point. The pattern is completed by a third bar, which indicates that the downward trend will continue even further. This pattern has also had a fair share of accuracy, and it is a pattern that any day trader wants to look out for.

The Abandoned baby: This is a bullish reversal pattern that usually is at the bottom of the low of a downward trend. The next is a Doji candlestick that shortens the market gap. It is followed by a bullish gap as the third bar, which completes the pattern and helps to indicate that the increase in prices will most probably rise higher in an upward trend. This pattern has had a high degree of accuracy, and it has helped various traders.

The major variation from the main candlestick strategy is the engulfing candlestick strategy. It allows the trader to get into trending moves whilst the momentum picks up. Similar to the simple candlestick technique, the engulfing candlestick has both the bearish and bullish patterns. An engulfing bullish (green) candle is one whose body of the up candle totally wraps over the body of the prior down candle. On the other hand, a bearish (red) engulfing candle is one whose wide part of the down candle totally encloses the wide part of the up candle. The wide parts are ones which indicate the close and opening of the trade. A large down candle followed by a larger up candle indicates that the direction has shifted significantly. This trend creates a powerful strategy of trading, having predicted the right direction.

The best way of working with the engulfing candle strategy is by using it together with a trend. After establishing the dominant trend, then you can tell the right direction to adapt when trading. There are two main types of trends, an upward and a downward trend. The former occurs when the price advancing waves are bigger than the price pullback waves, making the market pricing progress. The latter occurs when the pullback waves are stronger than the advancing waves, which makes the overall process pullback more. Assuming long positions during an uptrend is advised while short positions are advised for downward trends. However, if no trend is observed, using this strategy is setting yourself up for failure.

Once the trend is established, the pullback should be observed, which allows you to get the opportunity to trade. A pullback should relate to the candle pattern, either bullish or bearish. Be sure to apply a stop loss order to prevent losses, since it is not always guaranteed that the trend will go on uninterrupted.

Benefits

The advantages of using candlestick strategy are that it offers you a competitive edge in the market, gives you strong buy and sell signals, and it is relatively easy to use. It makes the study of the current state of the market and the direction of price substantially easier. The market behavior elements that this strategy helps to identify are breakouts, consolidation, trend continuation, and trend reversal. Furthermore, the candlestick chart is visually appealing and easy to identify all trends and patterns.

Limitations

The major weaknesses of this strategy include that the candlestick looks different on every time frame. Most traders experience difficulty executing orders when using this strategy because although it is perfectly formed, the candlestick always looks different for every time frame that the trader uses. Traders would have to assume one timeframe to be able to follow this strategy for their benefit. Also, risk management, when using this strategy, can be somewhat difficult. Even if one places a stop order at the candle's low and enters on its high, how long the candle is going to be is highly unpredictable. If the candle closes beforehand or long overdue, then your risk-reward becomes substantially impacted. Nonetheless, these candles have been considered a sluggish indicator since traders will most likely execute a trade at the end of a candle, and other participants may need to move prices to benefit; hence limiting your chances of profiting.

Chapter 5: The Trend (Momentum) Strategy

Trading is all about momentum. Finding the momentum is among the first things new traders learn. The only way to make profits in any trade is when the prices are moving, i.e., when there is momentum. Different stocks move in different percentages at different times, but there is always a movement in the stock. Fong, Tai, and Si (2011) estimate that there will always be a stock moving at 20-30 percent, although sometimes it is more than that. Now, the trick that traders use to profit from trading is identifying the indicators that these movements share. For a momentum day trading strategy, the basic feature to look for is a moving stock. Further, the trader needs a float of shares, strong charts, high relative numbers, and to look out for any relevant news and reports, which act as a fundamental catalyst. Momentum trading is all about purchasing securities that indicate an upward price trend movement or short-term securities with a downward trend. Traders who use this strategy rely on the fact that whenever a momentum is established, chances are that it will continue. Whilst this shouldn't be the case in a market, historical records prove that this happens. Stocks that begin to rise tend to keep the trend for a long time, while those that are performing poorly deteriorate in the poor performance for a lengthy time.

Technical analysis is used to tell about the potential price of shares. Usually, the emotionally driven traders fall prey to traders using this strategy, since they trade based on the poor decisions of others.

Financial experts and economists explained the validity of the momentum strategy based on the efficient-market theory for a long time (Fischel, 1978). Common conclusions include that traders using this strategy take advantage of the weaknesses of other traders, including disposition, over or under reaction effect. Also, it is established that this strategy is especially fruitful for high-risk takers.

History of Momentum trading

Richard Driehaus, George Seaman, and HM Gartley were the first people to put momentum trading into practice back in the 1920s and '30s. They used this technique to manage their capital based on the ideology that a trader could earn more money by buying high and selling even much higher. They contrasted this approach to the popular ideology of buying underpriced securities and awaiting their prices to escalate. The basic value sought from this strategy was fast moving stocks that would allow reinvestment of the money earned into new stocks rather than holding down capital awaiting markets to determine when the stocks can be sold. The basic tenets of this strategy were, however, applicable as early as the 1700s by the great economist David Ricardo. He used this strategy to accumulate profits by purchasing stocks with a strong performing trend. Although its use began long ago, not much of the early history has been written about this strategy due to the scarcity of writing material prior to the 20th century.

The late 19th century is when the strategy's technical analysis gained momentum, and the great traders led by Richard Driehaus coined the trend following by introducing the basic elements behind the psychological cause and effect which could allow traders to observe the behaviors of their counterparts. What was and is still required for this strategy to work is entering positions on the basis of the movement, to hold onto these positions whilst observing the movement and to liquidate these positions on the same basis. The renowned traders in history argued that they held onto positions while they watched their profits rise.

Technical analysis tools

Successful execution of the momentum strategy depends on getting ahold of the main momentum. Technically, momentum trading entails buying recent winner stocks and selling recent loser stocks. It requires strict risk management tools to handle the overcrowding, volatility, and the hidden traps that may come in the way of profit attainment.

Therefore, a marketer has to know the main indicators to benefit from trend following:

- Trend line: It is the primary tool for measuring price movements. It connects two points of prices on a price chart. A line that is going up indicates a positive movement of the price, and traders are expected to leverage this to buy. On the flip side, a line that goes down indicates a negative movement, and this shows the trader that they can sell their securities.
- Stochastic oscillator: This a tool which analyses the pattern of closing prices of assets. A positive trend is identified by a closing price that goes near the high point, while a negative trend is identified by a closing price going near the low point.
- Moving average: This is a point which allows momentum traders to refrain from giving in to random price fluctuations. Price moving beyond this point shows that an upward trend is prevalent, and below this point, a negative trend is present.

Also, some of the rules that accompany the use of this strategy include:

Selection of security: When you are trading, you want to be sure that your strategy aligns with the type of security you trade on. In this strategy, traders are advised to select liquid securities because of their short-term nature and to avoid risks. Securities such as leveraged may not be accurate since they have a complex fund construction that may not give proper tracking. It is good to select those that trade high amounts of shares per day and have high floats, even though low floats can be leveraged when there are emotional reactions from other market players.

Risk management: Now, we know that risk management is among the basics of day trading. However, the simplified nature of trend following may lead to traders' poor judgment and decision making, leading to adverse failures. Some of the things you should not do include exiting a position late after saturation point, entering a position before a momentum forms since there may not be a momentum later, after all; leaving an open position overnight due to the occurrences of the night that might turn the momentum to your opposite direction, leading to losses; and if you are not alert to exit the trade immediately the momentum begins to take a reverse gear.

Managing positions: Position coordination is paramount when it comes to trend following because these momentums carry with them wide ask and bid spreads. This means that for you to gain maximum profits, momentum has to move far in your favor. The period for holding the securities should be carefully decided because staying in positions for long exposes you to greater risk. Whilst the position should be long enough to allow you to benefit, it should also be reasonable enough for you to avoid risks.

Exiting trade: As mentioned, it is paramount to exit a trade whenever you suspect the trend is about to take a reverse gear, although the basic key in this strategy is waiting for a reasonable amount of time as the trend moves higher. Now, it is important to exit your position whenever the price moves rapidly into an overextended state since this signals potential changes in the trend.

The variations from the main strategy

Absolute momentum: This is the technique in which the price of a stock is compared against its price in the previous period. The trader will most definitely enter a position using stocks that show a positive movement in prices.

Relative momentum: This is the situation where the price of a stock is compared with other stocks within the market. Usually, momentum traders will choose to trade with the stock that is performing stronger than others.

Advantages

One good thing about this strategy is that traders are not concerned about the performance of a company since it is a short-term strategy.

Also, it gives high profits over a short amount of time. At times, a trend may have prices shoot rapidly over your intended holding period, and there is the potential of making even up to 50% returns on your invested capital. Also, it performs much better than other basic trading techniques, since factors such as time, asset class, and geographical location do not really matter. Using this strategy, you are able to maximize on the volatility of the market, since you look for securities that have an upward moving trend. Also, it is relatively easy to use and worthwhile, as its history has proven its workability.

Disadvantages

The major limitation and the reason why this strategy has been overly criticized is that it contains with it high risks for the periods when it just doesn't work. Just the way a momentum gets better by the day, if a stock you are trading on gets a bad momentum, then you are on the losing edge.

Also, this strategy is arguably expensive because the high turnover on stocks usually incurs high fees. Furthermore, this strategy consumes a lot of the trader's time in waiting for momentum to form and also waiting for the highest potential of the momentum once it forms. Nonetheless, this strategy is market sensitive since momentum forms when prices are rising. A downward trend does not favor this strategy.

The mainstay of the momentum/trend following strategy is to not be the trader on the side that is taken advantage of. There are various traders being controlled by emotions, no matter how many times they are told that emotional responses are an enemy in the trading scene. If you are controlled by emotions, you can't be a good momentum trader, since other momentum traders who are alert will take advantage of your emotional decisions.

Furthermore, various traders are practicing this strategy on a professional level, thus as an individual trader, perhaps working from home, it may not work for you. You may lag behind and become overtaken by the professionals who have mastered the art of getting news and reacting to it instantly. Technically, failure to act right on time in this strategy leads to overall losses.

Chapter 6: The ABCD Pattern

THE ABCD pattern is an indicator that detects the rhythm of the market movements, helping traders to know when to enter and exit positions. It is a part of the harmonic group of patterns alongside others such as cipher patterns and Gartley. It is interchangeably used for AB=CD. It is one of the simplest patterns to identify on a trading chart.

As its basic chart indicates, the ABCD pattern indicates a price action that begins at point A moving in a new direction, then reaches point B and makes a swing, retracting down to level C, then resumes the same length of the leg created by AB, up to point D. When the AB leg equals the CD leg, a price reversal from CD is expected. This gives a confirmation to traders that they can rely on the pattern to enter positions right after the reverse of the CD price move.

History

The ABCD pattern is a relatively new strategy as compared to others discussed above. It can be traced to the teachings of the founder of Harmonic Trader.com. He is known as Scott. M Carney and he established the Harmonic trade approach in the 1990s. His idea was to develop a system of the recognition of price patterns, which has been popular in the past two decades. Whilst there are other conventional chart patterns that are great powers in identifying market trends, the ABCD has also proven its great potential in understanding and leveraging the volatility of the market.

Types of ABCD Patterns

Bearish ABCD

A bearish pattern is one in which the pattern begins with a low price that climbs up, then takes a swing to drop. The bearish line AB is reversed by BC, which then reaches CD. Notably, point D goes beyond the first point created by B. Such a pattern indicates that price swings will continue to take place.

Bullish ABCD

For a bullish pattern, the first price point is at a higher point (A) to the point where the first swing takes place (B); hence the pattern that forms is one in which the prices go down then rise. In a bullish chart, the CD leg goes at a much lower point than that created at B initially. However, a price reversal at point D is expected, and this means prices are rising.

Rules for trading with the ABC pattern

The unique chart for the ABCD pattern implies that

there is a unique set of rules for trading with it:

Entry point: The first thing that a trader does when entering a position is to confirm the validity of their strategy. Therefore, to confirm that the ABCD pattern is really valid, you have to identify two reversals parallel to each other and of equal length. If these features are present in the chart, then you are set to enter a position at the point when the CD leg takes a reverse. Also, you should be keen to follow the direction of the price move that is counter and not parallel to the CD leg. Hence, you should be keen on establishing whether it is a bearish or bullish pattern since for either of them you enter in a different direction from the other.

Stop loss: Now, we know the significance for stop-loss orders, since despite how accurate you are in entering a position, there is always the probability of the market taking a wrong move, contrary to your expectation. Hence, it is always safe to include a stop loss order to be more prepared to evade loss. For the ABCD pattern, the appropriate stop loss position is the point above the extreme formed at the end of the extreme CD leg. Noteworthy is that the trade entry point and the stop loss point are very close to each other since the trade is entered at the beginning of a new trend.

Take profit: In the ABCD pattern, the minimum target for any position that you assume should be a move which equals the CD leg length. In this case, since you enter the market at the point where the CD move began reversing, the price move that comes after this reversal of trend should reach 100 percent retracement of CD, or in simpler terms, it should equal CD in length. However, as a trader, you definitely want to maximize profits, and it is always good to remain open to maximization. Therefore, since a length which equals CD is the minimum profit point, the length could extend further, and by keeping your trade open, you could catch higher profits.

For the tactical traders, they wait until the price move attains the minimum target and close about 50 percent of their trade and keep the rest trying to catch the profits from the continuing trend. This is a way of spreading risks and at the same time making the most out of a single trade. While awaiting the maximum price, a trader should always keep their eyes open for any emerging news and chart patterns that could indicate a potential shift of direction. If there is enough evidence that the trend could take a negative turn and affect your trade, you should act promptly to close even the remaining 50 percent and avoid impending losses.

Essentially, the ABCD pattern is the foundation of all other charts and patterns in the market, since they all follow price movements from a particular starting point to another.

Advantages

The fact that the entry point and the stop loss point are very close to each other means for the trader that there is a great win-loss ratio. Once you get it right when entering a position, you can rest assured of worthwhile returns. The major thing you do is look out for when to exit a portion of your position and leave the rest in the market awaiting even greater profits. Also, this strategy allows the trader to know the risk and reward ratios beforehand, and the trader gets a good view of what to expect.

Disadvantages

There are various problems associated with the use of the ABC pattern. These include the fact that this strategy is subjective to the kind of harmonic leg that traders want to pursue. It's been mentioned from the beginning that subjective decisions always lead to poor results. For instance, any market consists of several impulse legs, and using subjectivity to select the one that you want is always going to result in a loss. Whilst the basis of this strategy is choosing the leg that coincides with the resistance structure, it is always challenging to choose the optimal leg amidst several legs.

Also, traders using this strategy expect that the market will see and respond to the patterns in their head, yet we know that the market never cares about your profitability or loss. You are on your own, and the market cannot change to your exact expectations. It only responds to the purchase and sale aspects.

Also, this strategy is more common in range markets, which may make a trader lose out on trending markets. It usually does not follow the trend, but goes against the trend, making the trader cut their trades often times. Nonetheless, in a range market, it is not always that you will get a harmonic pattern to leverage, and waiting to identify the right harmonic leg for you to invest wastes a lot of your opportunities in other stocks.

Enjoying this book so far? I'd love it for you to share your thoughts and post a quick review on Amazon!

Chapter 7: Reversal Trading

In finance, market reversal identifies as the situation in which the value of a stock goes back to the point it was at the beginning of the trading period. The prices in the market take a turn into the opposite direction.

Therefore, reversal trading is the change in the

direction of an asset's price. A reversal occurs in either direction, either downward or upward depending on the direction, the price had assumed.

Reversals often occur intraday, weekly, monthly, or even in a year, and they usually happen in quick paces. They are used by different traders differently based on their position duration. An intraday reversal is basically relevant to a day trader. A trend that is upwards is technically characterized by stronger high swings and weaker low swings, but if it reverses into a downward trend, the high swings are normally less strong than the low swings.

Indicators such as moving averages assist in identifying the possibility of a reversal. After setting the moving average, if the price is continuously moving above it, then the trend is continuing to move up, but if the price is moving below the moving average, then there is a likelihood of a reversal. Also, a trend-line that indicates the stronger highs that an upward trend makes is used in the case that if the prices get below the trend-line, then a reversal is likely to happen.

There are various reasons as to why reversals occur in the market, but the major reason will always be the forces of supply and demand, which are known as the major price determinants. Further, the forces of demand and supply are determined by a variety of factors in the market, including the adjustment of trade policy by the economic planners as they try to grow their economy or even as a result of changes in interest rates. Such factors act as catalysts that determine how traders indulge in the market, which further determines the direction of the prices of stocks.

History

The model of reversal trading is as old as the trading history since it is intertwined with the price action concept. Technically, price action entails an analysis of the price movements with the aim of identifying proper position entry and exit points. It is usually not concerned about the actual performance of a security but takes into consideration its price movements. It is all about the actions of the price of a security.

This strategy has withstood the test of time since various credible authors have written and highlighted various benefits of this form of trading. Most of them base their sentiments on the real case scenario in the market and offer valuable insights to traders. They accredit it to various wins in the trading history.

For instance, Mark Fisher, in his *The Logical Trader,* discusses credible techniques for analyzing the market volatility and its potential high and low points. Fisher discusses ways of identifying the potential price changes to act on a position. He gives rise to variations of the basic trend reversal strategy, with the most relevant being the sushi roll. As its name suggests, this technique was discovered by a group of traders over the lunch hour. This technique is explained using a five-bar scenario, whereby the first 5 bars have weaker highs and lows, while the remaining 5 have stronger highs and lows. The last 5 usually engulf the first 5 in a bearish kind of pattern. If it is present in an upward trend, the sushi roll indicates a strategic long position selling, while in a downward trend, it indicates a potential reversal of price trend. The major drawback with this variation strategy is that the ability to capture this pattern is limited because the sushi roll must have 10 bars. This is unlike the engulfing bearish strategy, which normally has two bars and is easy to spot in a chart.

Another strategy variation is the outside reversal strategy, which is basically the sushi roll but that which uses data daily from Monday to Friday. It is even harder to achieve since it requires that the first five days in the week record lower highs and lows, while in the second week the five days record an outside engulfing with weaker lows and higher highs.

Advantages

It is among the best strategies to leverage to identify the strongest price trends. It is a simple strategy to follow, and you don't necessarily have to use indicators for you to see a trade signal. The price is the major indicator. In fact, most traders who try to introduce other external indicators often beat themselves in their own game. This is especially the case for the traders who think that indicators have to be used without actually serving a real function. Further, it has relatively high profitability, since it is all about getting a reversal pattern, and it is given that all price trends eventually reverse at some point. It is in the reversal trading that huge gains are found. Even though it has higher risks than simple strategies such as the trending technique, the higher the risk in reversal trading, the greater the returns. It only requires a disciplined trading model that is able to handle the risk involved.

Disadvantages

One major drawback of using this strategy is that it is difficult for the trader to establish whether price changes are minor and stay abreast of all the noise in the market. Most often, reversals are fast-paced, and traders fail to recognize them beforehand and act quickly to avoid losses. This happens even while indicators are rightfully placed, and it is often beyond the control of the trader.

Further, the market often has fake signals that a reversal is possible. Prices may go totally below the indicator, which means that there is a reversal, but it may resume immediately to the prior trend. Even if the reversal resumes its initial trend, the traders have already experienced their fair share of losses if they had not withdrawn from their positions.

Overall, the key elements of reversal trading include that traders attempt to exit positions in which a reversal is possible, or when the reversal is happening to avoid losses. It basically shows that the price of an asset has changed from increasing or decreasing in the opposite direction. Usually, the price changes that matter are the high margin ones, and the small changes in prices, also known as consolidations or pullbacks, do not have much effect on the trade.

Whilst a reversal is a total change in the price direction of an asset, a pullback is usually a countermove that does not necessarily reverse the price direction. Pullbacks are the situations which create stronger lows in the upward trend, and a reversal does not occur until the prices go below the indicator, say, trend-line, that the trader is watching. One thing to be keen on is that reversals often begin as potential pullbacks, and before you know it, it has started, and it is too late for you to act.

Finally, reversals are a must in the trading scene. No price takes a particular direction for the rest of its trading time. At some point, a reversal is expected. Therefore, the sooner one understands these reversals, the better it is for them as traders.

Chapter 8: The Scalping Strategy

It is among the most common strategies in the trading sphere. Traders rely on this broad strategy to benefit from little changes in prices. It fits users who have great position exit strategies. It also requires traders to make several trades in a day to make a profit. Also, it requires a proper technical analysis on a real-time basis since it basically refers to the mechanism of holding positions for the shortest time possible. Failure to capture the position and trend of the prices of the stock you are trading in could cause massive losses, which eliminate other various small gains you may have accumulated.

This strategy is based on the ideology that any stock completes the first phase of the movement, after which some stocks do advance further, while others do not. Therefore, a scalping trader focuses on the number of trading results and not the size of the wins. This strategy contrasts directly with the *let your profits run* perspective. The latter identifies as the situation where traders focus on optimizing the wins by increasing the winning margin while letting some other trades reverse. Thus, while some traders win through about half of their overall trades in a period on a long time frame because the wins are usually larger than the fails, the scalping trader has a potential of winning much more trades than they lose, although the wins are in small sizes.

Also, scalping can be used independently or can be used together with other day trading strategies. If it used independently, the trader enters several positions in a day and uses very short timed charts since the duration of the trading time frame is limited. The trader ought to have access to high functioning analysis systems and execute orders automatically. Most scalpers use the Direct Access Trading approach to get real-time information.

When used together with other strategies, the scalp strategy will come in as a supplement. Traders who focus on longer trends such as the ones discussed above can utilize the scalping strategy while awaiting their long trends to form. The trader enters in the longer time frame trade, and whilst it takes form, one enters into other tiny positions in the form of scalping.

Variations

There are a few variations to the main scalping technique. One is market making, which describes the condition where the scalp trader concurrently places bids and offers for a particular security. This strategy works for stocks that cause the least volatility in the market, and it is usually technical for a trader to compete with the market makers by being a bid and offer maker.

The second variation is when the trader buys several shares and looks out for a very small change in prices, usually a change as small as a few cents. This strategy requires highly liquid stock that is able to record changes in prices in quick successions.

The third is the scalp trading that looks almost like the traditional trading methods. A trader holds a position for any amount of shares as soon as the first signal is evident.

Fourth is the 1-minute scalping technique, which is perhaps the most popular technique in the scalping strategy. It was developed by a man called Paul Rotter when he placed various buy and sell orders frequently and made millions out of it. It particularly entails setting the chart on a one-minute timeframe.

Scalping techniques

That said, scalping is not the easiest strategy for beginners or inexperienced people, as it involves fast decision making and monitoring positions constantly, but there are some techniques that traders can use to benefit from scalping.

Order execution: A beginner would have to master the art of fast execution since a delay wipes out any accumulated profits. Order execution has to be accurate to make up for the limited profit margin per position.

Frequency and costs: This factor comes in the right from when the trader is choosing the brokerage firm, to when they are making trade decisions in every trading timeframe. Buying and selling stocks in the market accrues many commissions, which in turn have great impacts on the trader's profit share. Some platforms do not provide for scalping, and some charge a commission that may not be worthwhile when scalping.

Trading: The secret to all trading techniques is the ability to spot trends. This is even more important for scalping. Understanding the market price movement can place scalpers on the competitive edge since they do no stay in the position for very long and can benefit while the market is experiencing a slight boom.

Trading sides: The key to maximizing profits in scalping is balancing the long and short trades, but a scalper should especially maximize trading confidently in buying on the side.

Analysis: Now, we know that technical analysis is paramount for every trading strategy. To handle the high-frequency trades in day trading, traders should learn to analyze the market situation carefully and gain a competitive edge in the highly competitive environment. This is especially the case for scalping. You don't want to place your trades on a downtrend no matter how small the loss margin. You need to be careful to be able to gain as many small profits as possible.

Volume: In scalping, the high volume trades are often the most liquid, which is a good thing for the scalping strategy.

Advantages

The major benefit of the scalping strategy is that it limits the amount of exposure to the risk of a trader since one places small trades at small margins. Also, it increases the chances of winning, since making small moves is easily achievable. For traders focusing on big wins, there would have to be factored in the market influencing the actions of the traders heavily and hence increase market volatility. Further, a trader will always have something to do in the market, because even when the market looks relatively quiet, there are still small moves to be made.

Also, scalping comes off as a risk management technique in any trading system, since small trades can be taken within a major one to spread risks.

Disadvantages

The scalping strategy can be a disadvantage because of the fact that a trader needs a large deposit to be able to enter various positions. Usually, amateurs may not make much from it because they cannot leverage the market information like their dealer counterparts. Also, this strategy demands top-notch quality in mathematical skills, instincts, and automatic reaction to take advantage of the most lucrative chances. Additionally, it is time-consuming and may drain you mentally because of having to monitor the various positions that you have.

Overall, the primary goal of scalping is leveraging the sudden changes in the market and executing various orders in a quick manner. Since there are small gains obtained from each trade, you are expected as a trader to use above average leverages. The stop-loss order is highly workable in this strategy, so you can leverage these to avoid great losses. Even though it is the least risk intensive strategy, there is a need to have a profitable and solid strategy to use to gain the most out of it. Finally, it is certain that all traders enter the market to gain the maximum profits out of the trade. Remember that the scalping strategy gives small profits; thus, you have to work extra hard and enter as many lucrative positions as possible.

Chapter 9: Daily Pivots

Pivot points have for a long time been used by traders to determine the resistance levels of trades and provide critical support. The range-bound traders who maximize their trade on stocks that operate in price channels use the pivot points to establish the best position to enter and to identify the best breakout positions. They are useful for intraday trading, which has high-frequency trades. Prices tend to react to these pivot points, and they automatically set themselves up every day automatically.

There are various charting software programs in which the indicator can be customized. While some of these programs may allow you to have weekly or monthly pivot points, they are set on an ideal basis of one day.

The pivot point, also known as the average price level, is obtained by integrating the previous day's close, and the high and low points of the market as a function. This value is then divided by 3 to give out 3 support and resistance levels.

A wide range between these values leads to bigger distances between levels, and a smaller range gives a lower distance between levels. However, it is important to note that not all levels appear at the same time on the chart.

Once created, pivot points are the leading indicators to establishing the best turning point in the market, for identifying stop loss order positions, take-profit positions, and for entry or exit points.

Advantage

Pivot points are widely used in the day trading scene, although they were widely used in stocks and futures markets as well. The major advantage of pivot trading is that traders can use the pivot points as major indicators for getting ahead of the market. The position of the pivot is the central level on which every move within this strategy is evaluated. If a certain stock is trading beyond the pivot line, then there is a likelihood of the market trend for the day is bullish, although this does not mean that the trend can't take a reverse and trade below the pivot line. When there is minimal volatility in the market, the price of stocks revolves around the pivot line

Limitation

The major drawback for pivot points is their sensitivity to time zones. They are limited to the closing prices of London or New York's time. If a trader is using a different timeframe, then they have to be keen on the previous day's closing prices based on the strategy's basic time-zone. This drawback has often cost many traders because they plot different pivot points from the real situation in the market.

History

Similar to most other strategies, technological devices were not born by the time the pivot trading strategy was discovered. This strategy was discovered back in the day when traders need a way of keeping up with the relativity of market prices of stocks. This technique was born out of a mathematical equation. By taking the highs, lows, and closing of the previous marketing period, traders were able to find a framework for finding the 3 support and 3 resistance levels, as mentioned above. Traders depicted a reversal tendency when prices moved towards these levels, and if reversals did not occur, the traders would go ahead and look for the trade breakouts from the market prices.

Pivot points techniques

Gauging probabilities: Traders use pivot points to estimate the potential of the direction of the price being self-sustaining. There are certain estimates that seem to occur concerning how the price is likely to close the trading during the day below or above the levels. Although they are rough estimations, they often guide the trader in assuming a particular position when a certain estimate hits.

Stop losses: Pivot points are as well used as stop-loss orders, whereby a reversal is expected at some point. The stop loss level is normally the one above or below the reversal point in the case of a short trade and a long trade respectively.

Profit targets: The long term readings on a pivot chart indicator are used as a directive on how to take profits. Should the direction of the price move take a reverse, the trader is offered a good chance to exit their positions in an optimum manner and also to buy other stocks at a good price.

Breakouts: Whilst for most traders, arguably, high volatility is what guides their trading activity, the pivot point strategy equips a trader with the ability to spot support and resistance levels even when there is minimal volatility in the market. Each of these levels offers a chance for a day trader to enter positions in a highly liquid market since, after all, they do not hold these positions for longer than a day. The only drawback about using pivot points as breakouts indicators is that they tend to be more accurate for longer-term durations, say weekly or monthly durations.

Reversals: Although they happen less commonly than the breakouts, reversals are good indicators of prices going upwards or downwards. If the price is at a support level, then it is considered to have gone down, while if it is playing at the resistance level, it is considered to have gone up. It is always good for a trader to be sure that such an opportunity of buying low and selling high will occur before they can assume a particular direction.

Overall, pivot points are significant for viewing the likely resistance and support levels in the market. This helps traders to approximate the points where prices can overturn or consolidate. They are appropriate for day traders and can be leveraged using a combination of analysis tools and indicators that inform decisions.

Final thoughts about strategies

Whether you go for the automated strategies, the beginner strategies, or the advanced strategies, there are some basic components that every strategy should have. These include volume, volatility, and liquidity. Every strategy should be able to show you how much given security has been traded over a certain timeframe. This is, in day trading, referred to as the daily average trading volume, which tells you how much traders are interested in the asset. This can give you insights into whether or not there is a likelihood of good performance with the security. A high volume definitely indicates that traders are highly interested in the asset. Second, a good strategy should allow you to see your potential range of profits, based on market volatility. High volatility, as aforementioned, means that the prices can move quickly down and they can also shoot high, making the profit/loss margin potentially high. Also, a good strategy will allow you to trade on the stocks you find most liquid without limitations. Such stocks could include natural gas and oil.

Note that for the extensive learning on the strategy you decide to settle on, you can leverage videos and texts to increase your chances of understanding the content. Clearly, every strategy discussed above is suitable for different traders at different times. Once you identify yourself as an individual, you can establish the best trading strategy that suits you. Finally, being consistent with your strategy and making the best out of it is what it takes for success.

Section 3: Completing Your Trade

Chapter 10: Building a Watch List

In this context, a watch list is a list of stocks that you would prefer to trade, or rather those that fit your trading approach. You may term it as a list of securities being monitored for investing opportunities or potential trading. There are thousands of issues in each stock market, for instance, US stock exchanges list more than eight thousand issues. However, traders concentrate on a fraction of the securities. It can be agreed that identifying the most suitable stocks is challenging and requires a skilled trader. Exposing yourself to various aspects related to establishing favorable securities will play an important role. The first requirement for having a good watchlist is understating the modern stock market environment. You should understand how various sectors respond to catalyst overtime and how various levels of capitalization affect price development.

Importance of building a watchlist

As mentioned, there are numerous stocks listed in various stock markets such as Nasdaq and NYSE - to total is estimated to be more than eight thousand. Truthfully, it would be a challenge to keep up with that high of a number of stocks. Even the highly educated, experienced, and those with access to much information would find it difficult to keep up. Having a watchlist will help you identify potential trades that meet your trading strategy or criteria.

It is a reliable tool to use, regardless of the trading approach you use. It means that you have narrowed down to specific stocks or securities to observe attentively. Identifying suitable security requires more information, or rather reading beyond the promotion and message board. Lack of preparation has been identified as the key reason why more than 90% of traders lose money. Thus, a watchlist filters a number of stocks that you will focus on when trading. Thus, it will help shape your concentration and focus, which are essential aspects when it comes to trading.

When you are focused on a certain number of stocks and securities, it makes you ready so that you can quickly react if and when a trade's signal triggers. it is important to know that stocks can trigger trade signals simultaneously, and if you delay, there is a risk of missing entries or exiting. You can look at a watch list as a tool to prepare you ahead of time and a weapon to curb delays in the case of signals. In focusing on a few stocks, it is possible to capture and anticipate moves early enough. Another advantage is that a strong watchlist enables you to diversify your opportunities when trading. The mistake that most traders make is spreading too thin with many stocks and impulse jumping to any trigger. It results in revenge trading, impulse trading, and over-trading.

How to build a stock list

When you are seeking to build a stock list, you will need to keep in mind various considerations. One of these is to note that you are looking for stocks that meet your trading strategy or criteria. Also, it is important to consider the amount of time that you will be dedicating to trading and observing the financial markets. If trading is part-time, it is recommendable that you keep things simple by having a list of 50 to 100 issues to observe, track, and trade every day. If you are a committed trader or a professional, you can have a primary database that contains between 300 to 500 stocks.

Trading screens are important components in stock trading. As a trader, you have to decide on the number of trading screens and the form of stock charts that they display. The general rule points out that a trading screen can hold twenty-five to seventy-five stocks depending on market depth windows, news tickers, scanners, and space that charts take. You can choose to dedicate a given screen to tickers which show percentage change, net change, and last price.

We noted that you need to know the stocks that meet your trading criteria. It means that you will keep in mind the following things about a stock before including it in your watchlist.

Company details

You will need to know what the company is, what it does, and/or its market portfolio and market reputation. Although trading is different from buy and hold stock investing, it is important that you be conversant with the company aspects.

Stock analysis

The stock analysis involves fundamental analysis and technical analysis, all relating to searching for information about a given stock. The traditional stock analysis involves learning the history of stock trading. When doing fundamental analysis, it will entail learning about the business and its environment. The essential tools when doing fundamental analysis include the overall financial position documents as well as Securities and Exchange Commission filings. Most people avoid fundamental analysis on the notion that it is tiresome and time-consuming. However, you can greatly benefit from the information it provides. In doing technical analysis, it will require you to know the recognizable patterns, current price trend, and historical price movement of stocks. When analyzing, you should look at the stock with the biggest percentage gains from the previous day. It should be followed by looking at chart breakouts.

Interesting and most suitable stocks to choose are earning winners and contract winners. The advantage of identifying which stocks fall in the noted classifications is that one does not need to comprehend complex financial statements. For instance, you can search for stock spike, which is simple to identify. When looking for contract winners, you can search for the press release of small companies that are signing deals with big companies. If the deal is legit, then there will be a spike in its stock price. Also, trading volumes are good indicators of a possibly good stock. As a trader, you should stay away from a company whose stock has fallen by a significant percentage, such as 50 percent in a day.

At this point, you have equipped yourself with important information about potential stocks that you can trade. To avoid spreading yourself too thin, it would be good to limit yourself to five to ten stocks. It should begin with the strong to the weak market sectors. Also, you have to ensure that each of the stocks included in the watchlist has potential trade triggers, ensuring that you have planned the trade triggers ahead of time. This is why you considered the stock in your watchlist. Prior planning will entail having the legwork done in the pre-market to ensure that you will be ready when a given trigger forms. We noted that a trigger is that which determines whether you will buy or sell a given stock. Experts in the market describe a suitable stock as "shovel ready." The implication in this is that you can immediately take a given action on a stock when an indicator triggers.

Also, we noted that a watchlist entails those stocks that fit your trading strategies. You should actualize this by ensuring that you are honest with your trading style. Take, for instance, an intraday scalper. For such a person, the most suitable stocks will be those that follow through and have good momentum and volatility. Also, those stocks that are gapping on a catalyst event or on the news are best suited for such traders. How will you carry out good scalping? The best way to do this will be by implementing shorter time frame charts. A swing trader will focus on different things. These include targeting less volatile and slow moving stocks because they allow for longer holding periods.

Other important considerations are liquidity and volume. While you may wonder why you should bother with these aspects, it is important to note that volume to a certain degree ensures liquidity, while liquidity supersedes price. A good or tradable stock is that which meets both conditions, as they prevent you from being disadvantaged. You should avoid a stock that has no volume. In doing so, you are proving to be selective to the best opportunities. In doing this, you will have to ensure that you do not waste time on mundane prospects.

The other trick is to set alerts for intraday and swing trades. It is not as complex as it sounds, because most charting programs and trading platforms allow the users to set alerts. It has proven to be a reliable technology because constant monitoring of stocks could be tiresome. You can set alerts depending on indicator triggers or price. However, ensure that you separate swing trade alerts from day trading alerts. The essence of alerts is that they allow you to maximize your focus when needed.

When you have implemented the noted guidelines and familiarize yourself with trading, you will realize that you are well versed with information. With time, you will see that your watchlist is growing large. At this point, having multiple and diverse watchlists categorized differently is beneficial. The categories may include long-term investment stocks, sector plays, swing plays, and short-term stocks.

Chapter 11: Paying Attention to the Market Until the Trade is Completed

Self-sabotage has been established as one of the major drawbacks for a trader. As aforementioned, it is usually the errors that traders commit, which lead to losses, and not the method that they are using. However, most traders want to pick a method and run it in the market without efficient coordination, yet still, blame it on the method when they fail. One of the best ways through which you can avoid sabotaging yourself while trading is being keen on the market until the trade is over.

One of the biggest and longest-running traders in history, Peter Bandt, compared day trading to a marathon race. The main focus of a marathoner is getting to the finish line. Marathoners do not lose their focus until they get to the finish line and the ones who give in to distractions along the way, or listen to people's comments, or even doubt themselves never win. The reason why day trading is compared to a marathon race is that its positions are short-lived, yet entail a very eventful time period. How well you maintain your focus on your set time periods for holding a certain position determines your performance in the trade. Focus maintenance most often is the distinguishing factor between winners and losers in day trading, just as is the case in the marathon race.

Some of the ways through which you can maintain your attention while day trading is:

- Make small and manageable watchlists: Truth be told, you are bound to have too many items on your watchlist, which will make it hard for you to remember them all at various points in our trading times. At times, there are too many active and ripe stocks for you to trade, and you may get confused in the midst of creating your intraday trading goals. Typically, no one wants to miss out on any hot plans in the market. However, when you want too much, you end up losing it all. We are all human, and our concentration is bound to get lost when we are trying to handle too much. Therefore, indicate the items that you want to focus on in a day, so you are assured of not losing focus once you enter a trade. There is still tomorrow, and you can try different options. After all, each day brings with it unique fortunes.
- Use a few technical indicators: Whilst indicators are among the crucial requisites for success, they can be harmful if not well used. Using a lot of them denies you the opportunity to maintain your focus on the trade, since all the time you will be shifting from one indicator

to another trying to capture what you are supposed to do for each indicator. In the midst of this, you might lose concentration or just get exhausted and lose your focus.

- Define your trading style wisely. Whenever you set out on a journey, you have to know what you need. You have to know how you are going to handle anything that might come your way while trading. Most importantly, you must have a blueprint that you follow in your trading journey. In a market characterized by many players, platforms, strategies, and techniques, you have to define your style really wisely, lest you won't be able to pay attention to one trade that you enter. This is discussed in detail in the minimalism approach section below. It is built on the perception that most often, more does not mean better. A simple style can allow you to focus until your trade is over.
- Avoid the noise in the market: As already mentioned, most of the messages you get are pure noise while in the trading market. Everyone in the trading scene can start a rumor, under or over-analyze a small issue, and it can come up in your way, making you lose your focus. However, be sure to follow your intuition and model without getting distracted from your trade until it is over. When you are focused, you know how to distinguish between messages that are valuable for your trade and those that are not. You will ignore all rumors and follow your trading plan.

- Eliminate any distractions: Just like in any other job, distractions are a major threat to maintaining your focus on a trade until it is over. As aforementioned, we are living in a world full of distractions, especially those brought by the technological communication devices, with social media being a major distractor. Having the power to avoid being distracted while you have an ongoing trade is critical to your success. It is not easy to multitask and have a sustainable focus. It is not easy to keep browsing your social media platforms and still be able to give your ongoing trade the focus it needs.

Chapter 12: Day Trading Tips for Success

Day trading is considered to be among the most hyped yet misunderstood styles of trading. People often confess to hearing a lot of myths and misconceptions surrounding the practice, and it is worth identifying credible tips concerning what it takes. As stated, day trading involves the purchase and sale of stock within the same day. A position held overnight and longer is not considered to be day trading. Among the tips that significantly help achieve success include:

Identify Key Entry and Exit Points

In the trading spectrum, there is usually the price at which a person enters a trade. The point is usually referred to as the entry point, and it is considered best if it is backed up by a research-based strategy. The entry point is typically similar for all traders and is usually at the point at which the stocks are their low points.

As is common with shares, the par value changes in accordance with many factors. There are different ways through which one can identify key entry and exit points:

- Using the pivot point, support, and resistance strategy. The pivot points are usually calculated using the open, high, low, and amounts at which the stocks closed during the previous day. The pivot point usually uses a short-term time frame as well as a standard pivot point to calculate the points. To begin, one can open a one-minute OHLC (open, high, low, and close)[1] bar chart from the specific market and add the daily pivot points. Once open, one then waits for the price to move towards a pivot point, indicating the highs as they proceed. One is then supposed to wait for the price to touch the pivot point, which means that the price is trading at the pivot point price. This is the point at which one should trade at, buying shares from the companies which they wish to.
- The next point is usually waiting for the trade to exit. This usually involves waiting for the price to trade at the targeted price as well as the stop loss. The pivot point usually changes after a very short time and can take anywhere from a few minutes to several hours for one to reach their target. Depending on the market being traded, the target time is not defined, though knowledgeable day traders are usually able to discern and predict the most likely times for the trade to exit.
- Lastly, repeat the steps as many times as possible, until either the daily profit target is

reached or until the market is no longer active.

Avoid Hitting and Running

To succeed in day trading, hit and running must be avoided at all costs. The approach usually involves a person entering the market at its high, then exiting when it declines. The people who use this strategy are usually interested in making sudden huge profits and, typically, take immense risks using the strategy. These people focus on what they consider to be "sure bets," placing a huge amount of money on stock while at its lowest and selling when it attains the highest point in the day. The traders never concentrate on particular stocks and shares, but rather determine the stocks which they would want to deal with in the morning.

The biggest disadvantage with this strategy is that it restricts the traders from growing in their trading craft. Hit and run traders always attempt to play it safe and do not really follow the tenets of trading as they should. Therefore, they do not advance to the real trading scenario, which teaches people a lot of the skills necessary to earn immense profits. Also, sticking to specific markets may enable traders to be able to learn all they can about specific companies, thus enabling them to be able to predict expected changes when certain events occur. In such a case, the traders are better suited to organize their finances and plan towards devising strategies that would enable them to make the maximum profits.

Limit Losses

One of the basic rules that supersede all others in the quest to excel in day trading is limiting losses. As is known, day trading is a game of probability, where there is always the possibility of making profits as well as making losses in equal measure. Despite the fact that sometimes it is impossible to prevent losses, there are a number of strategies that can be used to improve the chances of success while significantly reducing the chances of accruing losses.

The first step towards limiting losses is analyzing and determining the expected returns on all of the trades that one is considering. Calculating the expected returns of all of the trades that are being considered enables one to compare the results and choose the ones that promise and offer the most opportunity for profit. The formula that is normally widely used in the calculation of expected returns is:

Expected Return = [(gains probability) x (The take Profit % investment Gain)] + [(loss probability) x (Ending Stop Loss % Loss)][2]

Another vital way through which trading losses can be managed is through the strict management of the risks possible on individual trades. A good rule is that a good trader should refrain from risking more than 1% of their balance in one trade. An example is a situation where one has $10,000 in their trading account. To manage their risk, they should not risk more than $100 in a single trade. It is always worth noting that one can have extremely bad days in trading, and investing minimally ensures that they never have to lose everything on a bad day.

Creating a daily stopping point is also vital for risk management. A good trader always knows when to invest and when to stop. When a trader is coming up with the daily trading strategies, they must always decide how much they can afford to risk each day and the point at which they must stop. For instance, a person can decide that they will always stop when they lose a certain percentage of their investment, say 3%. Some people also decide to stop when they lose a certain number of times in a row. Most traders assert that when they decide to stop based on their average profits, the overall amount that they can afford to lose always grows significantly over time. Skills develop significantly using such strategies.

Also, creating limit orders helps to keep losses at a minimum. Using limit orders is also considered to be a great strategy of limiting losses in day trading. The limits are mostly used for buying and selling. Buy limits only purchase stocks which are below the limit price and sell limits only sell stocks when they are above the limit prices. The best way to limit losses is always to create a plan and stick to it. Day traders must always be very vigilant and stick to their orders to benefit.

Starting Small

Day trading, when done right, is one of the best ways through which people can invest and gain financial freedom. Most of the successful day traders whose investments run into millions assert that one of the strategies they used is starting small. Regardless of the amount that one has, they can put in into an investment and start earning. Currently, it is possible to begin investing with as low as $100. When the traders combine other aspects such as being open to learning as well as learning as much as they can about the trading process, they can enjoy wins that accumulate over time.

When one is just starting out, it is always imperative to diversify investments so as to ensure that they do not lose their initial income. Small day traders are usually advised to focus on small yet reliable profits. The small hits always have the capability of adding up to much bigger gains over time. As the profits increase over time, one is then in a position to take much bigger risks and consequently pool in more money for individual trades.

Willingness to learn

Just like any other craft, day trading has distinct strategies and procedures that help improve chances of success. Experts assert that people exempt from studying do not have what it takes to be profitable traders. There are very many practices and new modes of operations that come up each and every day, which improve the chances of success for traders. Learning about the new and emerging modes of operations is beneficial since it keeps the traders on the forefront of the credible trends as realized with the changes in the trading patterns. Willingness to learn entails being humble and acknowledging that there are things you don't know. With such a mentality, one can be open to learning, as well as devise strategies which will help them grow over time. There are experts who have been in the game for a long time and can give invaluable advice to aspiring listeners. One cannot grow without listening to advice from experts, hence the need for a willingness to learn.

In addition to the expert advice, the traders need to learn that different events affect the values of shares significantly. There is usually the need to learn how to discern events that affect the trading prices from the onset. For instance, whenever scandals hit a certain company, its share values drop significantly. With proper discernment, the traders can be able to predict which shares will regain their value as well as those who cannot recover under any cost. The traders are then better suited to purchase the stocks which will recover since they will make an undoubted profit. For the stocks which are likely to decline, even more, the traders should keep off their purchase. Traders who are willing to learn about discernment are able to make the right decision during all transactions.

Risk only what you can afford to lose

One of the smartest pieces of advice that new day traders must acknowledge is that one should only trade with the money which they can afford to lose. As is known, there is always the possibility of gaining as well as an equal chance of losing. Trading may go sour, and a person is always likely to lose all of the investment that they made. Therefore, it is immensely wise to only trade with what you can afford to lose. There are numerous cases of people falling into depression and even bankruptcy due to losing some of their livelihoods when they risk money that they need for their livelihood.

When investors know how much is at stake, they may end up confused and full of anxiety, which prevents them from making sober decisions. Some of the traders put the entire amounts in one share, consequently leading to a total loss when deals do not go through. Such huge losses are, in most cases, irrecoverable, and the result is undue depression and a life full of misery. Breaking up the money into a number of share investments increases the chances of gaining and leads to small losses when the inevitable occurs. As has been stated in the previous section, minimizing losses is imperative and a must for any trader who wishes to continue succeeding in the trading process.

Be realistic

Unrealistic expectations are one of the causes of failure in day trading. While the major goal of trading remains to be able to make profits, there are instances where traders may have unrealistic expectations. The fact that many people have become millionaires while trading does not mean that a person is bound to get rich overnight. Trading is usually a process, and sometimes, huge gains are the sole result of good luck. Therefore, it is not definite that a person will enjoy huge benefits at a go, and some people actually wait several years before they are able to make a substantial income.

Usually, the first step towards setting realistic goals is analyzing the statistics. In any business and any amount tradeable, there are always people who have traded before, leaving behind a trail of achievements as well as possible gains and losses. When the day traders study statistics, they are able to determine the extent to which they can achieve certain milestones as well as the potential losses for some investments. The data available is in the millions, and one only needs to log in to various databases and get the results that they would want.

The next step involves testing the mettle in a real life day trading sector. Currently, there are very many online platforms which have stock simulators and virtual trading platforms. The site involves simulators which act as they would in a real trading platform.

Potential day traders should first use the simulators, to get a feel for what they would achieve were they trading in a real platform. Through such simulators, the traders can then be able to make estimates regarding what they can earn and achieve in the real world, which enables them to set credible and realistic expectations.

Finally, as one grows into the real trading arena, they should track their progress periodically. In most cases, the traders are usually likely to identify strategies which work for them, and which enable them to have a successful run. When such strategies prove to be continuously beneficial to the trader, they can adopt them in future cases and be able to realistically determine the expected returns.

Timing the Trades

Trading is just like any other activity. There is always the best and the worst time to conduct it. Experienced traders know that there are certain days of the week as well as times of the day when it is considered to be the best time for trading. Some of the vital times which are considered to be ideal in trading include:

- Opening hours, which is the best time to buy stocks. The hour after the market opens is considered to be a highly volatile time since the buyers and sellers are reacting at this time. Established traders assert that the first 15-60

minutes are the best time to buy and sell stocks. The volatility that occurs in the accompanying hours is particularly challenging for new traders, and losses are increased.
- Established traders also assert that Mondays are the best time to buy most of the stocks. There is a well-documented tendency known as the "Monday-effect," which proves that most stocks drop on Mondays. Therefore, this remains to be the best time to buy such stocks since one increases the chances of selling them at a higher price.
- Fridays are considered to be the best day to sell stocks. Contrary to the Monday-effect, Fridays are usually the time when most of the people desire to unload the stocks that they bought throughout the week. Usually, most companies do not trade on weekends. Therefore, Fridays remain the last trading day of the week, and many brokers choose to sell on the same date.

Discipline

Just like any other craft, discipline is of the essence. Most day traders perform the trading tasks on a full-time basis, thereby making it one of their permanent sources of income. When the traders are immensely disciplined, they are able to go on with their trading practices unabated. Typically, traders are not restricted to certain companies and commodities but are able to trade thousands of products every single day.

Discipline also extends to following the day plans and strategies laid out. When the traders are able to follow strict guidelines and policies, they are able to prevent incurring losses by ensuring that they follow their safe methods of operation. Most importantly, traders require the discipline to be able to do nothing when there are no opportunities and be on high alert for potential opportunities. When the latter occurs, discipline is required to act instantaneously and keep a sober mind to ensure that the chances of losses are minimized.

Trading Plan

A trading plan is imperative to any business and any trading setup. As is commonly said, "failing to plan is planning to fail." Established traders assert that there are only two choices in their craft: either following a trading plan methodically or failing. Some of the tips which help in the creation of suitable plans include:

- Disaster avoidance. Trading is a business and must be treated as such. There are very specific elements that enable a person to be able to succeed in the craft. For instance, reading books, charting a program, and opening a brokerage account are not really plans. A plan is a determination of what amounts will be put up in a certain sector, the trading strategies to

be used, as well as knowing when to exit. The trading plans should be followed systematically and updated as one gains trading knowledge.
- A skill assessment must precede the preparation of a plan. Most distinguished traders normally test their skills out on paper before attempting to use them in the real world, so that they can have confidence knowing that the strategies actually work. Trading in the market is usually a matter of giving and take. Often, the traders operate on probabilities and are unsure about the outcome. When paper skills are confirmed, the traders are then able to operate comfortably in the real world.
- A good plan must always have a set risk level. Depending on a person's trading style, the risk level may range from a small percentage to a relatively high margin. By nature, some people are better risk takers than others. Therefore, one should identify the length to which they can go so as to be able to set their limits. You may also find that in some situations, you're willing to risk more than in others. Ensure you're always making logical and thought out decisions that are not based in emotion.

Chapter 13: Learning to Begin Day Trading with a Minimalist Approach

When all is said and done, it all boils down to what you do with your trading space. Trying to chew too much never proved beneficial for anyone, and neither did cooking too many pots at a go. Most traders struggle with trying to do too much at once. Absorbing too much information at once, understanding all trading concepts at once, trying out too many strategies at once, trading in too many platforms at once, or even entering way too many positions at once. Yet the quantity of what you do never matter over the quality of how you do it. It is in this connection that the concept of minimalists approaches to day trading crop up.

So what is minimalism, anyway? In general terms, minimalism can be described as the condition in which you intentionally acquire and only lead your life with the things you really need. Its basic tenets are intentionality, simplicity, and drive. It is your intentionality that makes you endorse the things that are most valuable to you while removing every other thing that distracts you from your purpose. The most successful people have one thing in common: they embarked on their journey, whether in sports, in business, or in any other area of their life, with a lot of focus and staying purpose-driven. Therefore, day trading is not exclusive to the minimalist approach.

In trading, a minimalist strategy is one in which you focus on those one or two things that work for you in the trading scene and growing your potential to trade day by day. It is about eliminating all the noise and maintaining your focus on perfecting a few skills that will help you edge the competition.

For traders, it takes quite an extensive time before you can really figure out what mistakes you've been making that do not necessarily have to do with your trading method but stem from the emotional mistakes that we can all agree have led us into errors at some point in our lives.

You need to ask yourself as a trader, the role that the clutter in your everyday charts plays in your failure to make it big. Just like our materialistic nature leads us into purchasing and acquiring things that we do not necessarily need but which arguably makes us feel fulfilled, the craze of learning how to trade drives you into making unthought-out moves that fill your plate with "*crap.*" The idea of having too many indicators and analytical tools, for instance, will obscure your judgment about a certain trade day.

The benefits of minimalism

Clarity of the mind: We already mentioned that the pillars of minimalism include clarity. Truth is, the connection between all the things that we try out, and our mental and emotional health is just magical. That magical feeling that you get when you clear that junk drawer in your kitchen is the same you should expect to feel when you cease employing way too many tactics in the trading scene. Remember that emotional state is core in making trade moves. Since minimalism gives you a chance to be clear about everything on your table, you should embrace this approach.

Too much monitoring of way too many prices moves stresses you and, eventually, you become unproductive.

Freedom: At the beginning of this guide, we saw that day trading is meant to be a form of financial freedom, and actually freedom to spend that money. It is not in any way meant to tie you down on a 24/7 basis. Yet it is so easy for day trading to hold you down every other time if you try tackling too many things at a go. Even the most successful traders in history never employed too many strategies at one time. In fact, almost all trading strategies were discovered by a different person. This is because when one discovered one approach, they focused on it and made it work on all levels. This way, you have time for trading and attending to your personal life.

Self-confidence: Since having a few indicators and trades in a day allows you to study them and learn every trick about them, this enhances your confidence in going about your trade, and you can be assured of making sound trading decisions. You begin to feel good about your overall life, which is an unexpected advantage of living with fewer things.

Purpose enhancement: When you are clear of the unnecessary things that you don't have to do in trading, a clear sense of purpose and goal achievement happens to you. You become motivated to trade on a daily basis because you have a clear direction, and there are not many alternatives confusing you. Having a few commitments motivates you to achieve them and see where you get with them. You can set daily milestones, look forward to achieving them, and then actually achieve them. Achieving the little milestones allows you to keep fetching wider profits progressively, handling each day at a time.

How to incorporate minimalism in your day trading approach

Now that we've seen the benefits of minimalism, the following is a checklist of some basic ways, you can incorporate the strategy in your daily trading strategy.

- Always start your day with a clean price chart. Do not dwell on trading robots for analysis, since these may obscure your trading day's judgment. Being able to start on a clean note calms your mind, and you will be able to focus

when analyzing the market.
- Concentrate on the simple price action strategies. Be sure to choose the simplest method of studying price movements, because this makes everything much easier than trying to look complicated like the trade gurus.
- Do not spend all your time analyzing the market every day. Rather, concentrate on creating quality analysis times that will give you a few workable signals.
- Do not engage in too many markets in a day. Instead, concentrate on enhancing your focus on the major markets, and this will ensure that you handle the markets like a winner.
- Refrain from the idea of fancy trading tools such as fancy computers or desks. As far as the minimalist approach is concerned, these are just added stresses that you are adding to your list. The best thing for you to do is actually buy what you can afford and not fill your working station with clutter in the name of being fashionable. Ensure that your trading station is clean and simple. You don't need 100 books on trading sitting around you for you to look serious. Bring minimalism to your surroundings as much as possible.
- Most importantly, eliminate any unnecessary things from your life that may be causing stress for you. Learn to cut off toxic and unnecessary relationships, do not indulge in day trading along with several other small businesses in the notion of income diversification unless you

have a trusted person taking care of your business, and do not have too much of a social media presence that might expose you to all kinds of rumors that may deter your thinking.

The key to making it big eventually is taking baby steps and being keen on every milestone that you arrive at every time. Before you can totally fix your feet on the ground, be sure to trade on about 3 stocks in a typical day and earn the most out of it. It is always better to start small and do really well on a few securities than be on the losing edge with many, whilst not learning anything at all. Minimalism is simply a secret code to living a happier and more fulfilling life in whatever you are doing. The basic idea here is to minimize what you put down on charts and maximize on a few tactics that work for you. Remember, the greatest failure in day trading does not come from the method you employ to trade. It mostly comes from the errors that you make while trading. Most traders are quick to assume that a method just did not work when really they did not take time to learn about the method and focus on trading fully with it. They simply learned about too many methods and added too many indicators as they think the gurus do, and they ended up beating themselves up. The thing is, a lot is not better than a little!

Chapter 14: Avoiding the Herd Mentality

Also, popularly referred to as the mob or the pack mentality, the herd mentality is a condition that describes how people are influenced by others in their decision-making process. Rather than their decisions being based on a rational idea, they are based on emotions because of the mob influence. Due to its increasing impacts in most people's lives and given its detrimental impacts to an individual's goals and purpose in life, the concept of the herd mentality has become increasingly studied as the experts and social psychologists attempt to create awareness among people.

The paradox of it all is that as a trader, you have all the reasons to get carried away by the herd mentality. As aforementioned, it is the herd mentality which prevented the masses of people in the Japanese rice trade from embracing the candlestick mentality. Muhenisa, who belonged to the small percentage of people that did not entertain this kind of mentality, leveraged the trading space and received many benefits out of it. We cannot deny that there will always be the masses who dictate what individuals do, and there are always those individuals who will follow the masses. In fact, the herd mentality is a strong force amongst our social lives, since all new fashion and norms are dictated on the societal level by the masses. It is hard to resist. However, it is this mentality that holds you back from joining the trading trend early enough.

Most often, it is usually the traders who go against the wave of the masses who make the most out of trading. The herd mentality lies to people and says that it is yet too early and unacceptable to buy stocks, and most people feel afraid of taking risks, and they settle with those sentiments. These people then miss out on lucrative opportunities of booming markets. In fact, most people fear day trading because the masses have it that day trading is all about losing your money and that it is a profession for the chosen few. They fail to embrace the goodness of day trading. Besides, the herd mentality is what makes most traders commit mistakes and end up losing their money, because they believe in rumors and execute orders in the market, which are wrongly led. One of the most recent detrimental impacts of the herd mentality is the 2008 housing bubble, which led to a crisis. It led to huge negative impacts from which economies are still struggling to recover. Every participant saw that the boom was bound to collapse, but because of the herd mentality, they continued being speculative and placed a lot of their cash in the market. You probably have come across news about the 2008 financial crisis even if you have not been a fan of news or economic trends since this topic has made headlines ever since. You know what happened. People lost huge amounts of money. Financial institutions collapsed, and money circulation was greatly interrupted. Those who might have been clever enough had exited the market and were safer with few or no losses, more than the masses who only decided to look at one side of the coin and thought the trend wouldn't change. Fast forward to know, and we know that successful trading calls for careful assessment of the market conditions, based on facts and not emotions. Being on the opposite side of this mentality helps you focus on what you can do to rock it in the market. It allows you to manipulate the vulnerability of others, which accrues from their herd mentality.

The average investor uses emotions to make decisions. They rely heavily on social trends. They manage positions based on the rumors going around and do not wait for the release of official reports or news to be informed in their next move. If all people in the market are interested in a particular stock, then most of the traders are likely to move in the same direction. Needless to mention, you should avoid the mob mentality if you really want to benefit from day trading. So many rumors and trends can arise in a single trading day and affect your judgment and decision making. But as one of the world's most prominent traders, Warren Buffett, would argue, you should be acquisitive when others are drawing back and draw back when others are overly acquisitive. Be sure to follow facts when making decisions and be your own master in the game. Do not be a slave to the herd mentality! You can do it!

Chapter 15: Reflecting on the Lessons Learned from Trading

When reflecting on the lessons learned from trading, it is important to note that the market has changed in the course of the years. As such, most of the tricks that traders used ten years ago may not be effective in the current industry setting. For instance, more than ten years ago you would have called in your buys and sell orders to your broker. This is not done anymore. People engaging in trading today meet a completely changed game. It is true that trading could be deceiving, and the best way to face the market is to be equipped with information, experiences, and lessons from those who have traded for a long time. The following are some of the lessons to learn from:

It pays to be a defensive-minded trader. A credible trader, Warren Buffett, developed a unique and famous quote. It states that a trader should have it as a basic principle to always strive to not lose money and to never forget this rule. The cautioning message in this rule is that as a new trader, one should not only focus on making money but rather try as much as possible to protect their money. The use of a defensive approach entails trading when your trading criteria have been met, not only when the market conditions are favorable. What you ought to know is that the goals of trading are not to lose money, but to make money.

The other key point of defensive trading is to preserve your trading capital. The implication of this is that as a trader, you will be able to maximize when an easy opportunity arises. This approach means having as much money as possible when an easy target or stork emerges. It means that a good trader will preserve their capital for an easy trade setup. These easy targets tend to have high probability price action signals that are obvious. Risk management is an important aspect of trading, and when you have properly considered its aspects as a trader, you will not be disappointed if you took a confluent and strong trading signal, but it failed.

Your last trade results should not affect your next trade. It is important to understand that results from your last trade have no effect on the next trade. It means as a trader, you should not be influenced by the last trade when making the next. You should know that every single trade you take is unique and different from the previous one. Although they may appear the same, it is important to note that the surrounding market context will be different. To affirm this, know that winners and losers are random when trading. For instance, if you make 100 trades in a year, you may end up with 50 losses and 50 wins, but the fact is the pattern is totally random. Or you could buy 5 losses followed by 1 winner followed by 7 more losers, and follow that with 30 winners. Noting this, the main question is - how will you handle the random nature of losses and wins?

The implication in this is that if you have decided to become a trader, be dedicated, confident, and a perpetual risk taker. These, among other qualities, will be key aspects in ensuring that any single trade will not distract you. If you let the results influence you, it will hinder you from realizing the real nature of trading. However, you need to be extra careful after a big winner. It is human nature to become overconfident and excited after a major winner or overly-fearful after a losing trade. Getting overconfident lures you into taking uncalculated and risky trading moves. The bad thing with this is that you may end up making losses. Trading through the influence of emotions can lead to wiping out your account in a day. So, it is important even after a big win to remain calm and make rational decisions.

Doing less trading activities could bring more: trading is not about doing too much, and most people who fall for this mindset are the new traders. However, it does not mean that conducting good research or watching the charts is wrong. Having a low-frequency trading approach has been accredited by the most successful traders. It may be debated with some pointing that this is a wrong lesson. What it means is a good trader should be able to filter the good trade signals from the bad rather than just jumping into action. You can do this by reading the footprint of the market. It will help in realizing the good stocks worth risking your money on. The mindset here is being cautious of the money you worked hard to earn.

Know where you are coming from before beginning to trade: As you have come to know in a trading business, you are the boss, and there is no authority above you. As such, quality of discipline and being able to hold yourself accountable are important. If you know that you are not self-controlled or disciplined enough, it is important that you develop these qualities first. You should know that exiting the market is harder than entry. A good trader removes himself from the trade exit process as much as possible. You should note that most traders exit the market based on emotion. In most cases, it results in large losses or small losses. It is true that it is harder to exit the market when it is favorable. The best course of action is to exit the market when it is in your favor instead of when it is cashing back against you because you will end up losing.

Master your trading strategy: while most people assume that they understand how to use the trading platform as per their trading strategy, this is not the case. You will find it a difficult trade when you have not adequately mastered your trading strategy. Look at it as trying to fly a plane while you have no training nor prior experience. Practicing your trading strategy will help you to get used to it as well as learn the most suitable tricks. You have to commit and master your trading strategy before the actual trading begins. Also, having one trading method is more helpful than having different trading methods. An additional component to this is having mastered your money management. You will do this by not increasing your trading amount until you see consistent success.

Master yourself: An excellent trader is the one who has already mastered themselves. As a trader, it is important to deal with the emotional or mental weaknesses that you have, because failure to do so will make it difficult for you to make money. Most traders fail to realize that success comes from going on a personal journey and conquering the pitfalls. You will do this by checking your ego. As a trader, being confident is an important quality, but being overconfident could be harmful. Overconfidence is also a weakness even to the greatest traders, which makes them make poor trading decisions. The aspect of overconfidence results from making several good winning trades.

Be disciplined: A good trader is a disciplined person. You may question the essence of discipline in trading. The element of being disciplined means that even after making a huge win, you will not do anything out of the ordinary. It is normal to feel wonderful or ecstatic after winning. But you should continue to trade as per your plan. As a strategic trader, your plan should provide for what to do after winning trades. An undisciplined trader, when they close a nice winner, tends to jump into the market and make another trade. Unfortunately, this turns out to be a mistake in most cases.

Employing confluence: In the context of trading,

confluence entails numerous supporting factors lining up to support the trades. The modern trading platforms have mechanical trading systems that have strict rules that they have to follow. The advantage with this system is it helps to eliminate human error. However, the best way to do this will require writing your trading plan well. You must have and adhere to a given trend, signal, and level agreement. For a beginning trader, a system like a robot trader has mechanical advantages. It will help you to build and improve discipline and confidence with your trading strategy.

Conclusion

Day trading is one of the most popular professions whose potential is overlooked. Most people consider day trading to be a profession where people just gamble or look to luck for their earnings. In fact, day traders are considered unethical. Most see it as a thing for the elite few who utilize mind games to take money from the naive players in the market. Yet day trading is just a unique profession, but with all the rules and principles of a typical profession. Profits in day trading are earned through every individual trader's efforts and tactics.

As discussed above, there are various reasons why you should indulge in day trading, including the fact that it gives you financial freedom, gives you a better overview of the world, it has a leveled playing field for all players, and it has life-enriching skills such as mental toughness and risk management. As a trader, you are forced to become the master of your own trade and get ahold of the best strategies to maximize your profitability. There are various strategies to be leveraged to make day trading work, and they all cater to different kinds of traders. Your day trading style is largely determined by factors such as capital availability, experience, and knowledge of the market.

Further, the basic start-up tools for a trader are relatively affordable, and it gives you the pleasure of working from the comfort of your home office or anywhere else. One of the most important things as a day trader is for you to ignore the herd mentality and not let it come between you and your trading intentions. Most people have failed because of over speculation or under speculation. Decisions in day trading require facts and not emotions; hence, you have to be stable emotionally and avoid being influenced by baseless rumors. Also, in day trading, you have to know how much risk you can take based on your qualifications and the nature of the market. The good news is that day trading is not something for the elite few. It is for everyone. You can become part of it, and you can attain big wins. Once in the market, your alertness, readiness, and consistency determine your victory or failure in the long-run. Just believe that you can do it and you will!

If you enjoyed this book or received value from it in any way, then I'd like to ask you for a favor: would you be kind enough to leave a review for this book on Amazon? It'd be greatly appreciated!

References

Abdolmohammadi, M., & Sultan, J. (2002). Ethical reasoning and the use of insider information in stock trading. Journal of Business Ethics, 37(2), 165-173.

Fischel, D. R. (1978). Efficient capital market theory, the market for corporate control, and the regulation of cash tender offers. Tex. L. Rev., 57, 1.

Fong, S., Tai, J., & Si, Y. W. (2011). Trend Following Algorithms for Technical Trading in Stock Market. Journal of Emerging Technologies in Web Intelligence, 3(2).

NerdWallet-Make all the right money moves. Retrieved from https://www.nerdwallet.com/

Ryu, D. (2012). The profitability of day trading: An empirical study using high-quality data. *Investment Analysts Journal*, *41*(75), 43-54.

www.ingramcontent.com/pod-product-compliance
Lightning Source LLC
Chambersburg PA
CBHW021824170526
45157CB00007B/2678